Sharon is tenacious, she is funny. Sh
Her book, her story will take you on
cry, and you will rejoice with her. Her story will keep you on the edge
of your seat. My prayer is that this will not just be a good book that
entertains you, but that her book will draw you closer to God, and that
through her story you will see the powerful force that drives her. Be
ready for uncut, raw, honest, funny, tear-jerking stories. Be ready to
laugh, to cry, to be inspired. Be ready to fall in love with her God.
Because without God there would be no story.

Pastor Alisa Gonzalez
The Master's House Church
Taree, NSW, Australia

What a brilliant read! I don't think I have read a book so fast. I cried in
the last chapter. It touched me, especially where you had put your Seer
gift on the shelf, but seeing how much the devil wanted to snatch that
from you. Holy Spirit is all over this book. Hearts will be unlocked and
lives will be filled with hope. A wonderful, real, honest testimony of
your life's journey. Thanks for being vulnerable and sharing, you truly
are a Daughter of the King.

Nawa Cooper
Nawa Cooper Ministries
Christchurch, New Zealand

This is a powerful testimony of God's grace.

Sarah Scott Webb
For Freedom, Anti-trafficking & Exploitation Ministries
SIM International

A brutally honest and raw account of a life relationship with oneself and the effects that it had on others. A journey of life before and after salvation to the discovery of a daughter of a King and His kingdom.

Pastor David Rua
Z Life Church, Selwyn, New Zealand

Sharon's honesty and transparency make this book so relatable to people from all walks of life. The struggles she has endured and overcome will speak to many to bring them to a place of victory in Him.

Pastor Lorraine Rua
Z Life Church, Selwyn, New Zealand

Sharon's story of God's sovereign intervention in her life during a random movie outing with a friend shows us the readers that nothing is ever wasted in His hands as He miraculously shows up and meets us right where we are in order to turn our wounds into a resource for his glory and for the extension of His kingdom.

Sharon has a gift in being able to paint a picture the reader can put themselves into. Her life journey of surviving to thriving . . . of discovering the Divine exchange of 'beauty for ashes' will inspire those who can easily relate and bring hope to those who are still 'sitting on the fence' stuck in their life narrative waiting to discover the treasures that God has placed inside of their 'clay pot' while longing to write the end of their story differently.

Jenny Purkis
Counsellor, Strengths finder Coach & Speaker
Merging Lives Counselling & Training

Having known the author, her husband and family for about fifteen years, when Sharon Reynolds sent me a copy of her book *Becoming a Daughter of the King* for a comment, I was thrilled to read about her journey. Sharon's journey is not unique, but as she has sought after God's will for her life, progress has been obvious to those of us who knew her. We delight in that progress, as well as the lives of others she has touched and assisted along the way. The impact Sharon has had on many people is very positive, and shows both God's grace and mercy, as well as Sharon's willingness to serve.

Becoming a Daughter of the King is very well written, and challenges the reader to consider what more they could be doing to aid others with their own journey. I have a hunch this will not be the last book Sharon will write!

Selwyn Stevens, Ph.D.
President, Jubilee Resources International Inc.
New Zealand

Sharon Reynolds has put her life on paper and written a book that is heartwarming, challenging and exciting to read. Her journey from brokenness to 'becoming a daughter of the King' is truly inspirational and life changing. Sharon has experienced the ups and downs of life, but her story reminds us that it only takes one encounter with Jesus for Him to change our lives forever. I highly recommend this book to anyone who is wanting a fresh touch from heaven.

Senior Ps. Luis Gonzalez
Endorsed Minister, Crosslink Christian Network
Taree, NSW, Australia

Becoming a

Daughter of the King

SHARON REYNOLDS

Torn Curtain Publishing
Wellington, New Zealand
www.torncurtainpublishing.com

ISBN Softcover 978-0-473-54157-6
ISBN Kindle 978-0-473-54158-3

Some names and identifying details of people described in this book have been altered to protect their privacy.

Scripture taken from the New King James Version. Copyright © 1982 by Thomas Nelson, Inc. Used by permission. All rights reserved.

Cover art by WHAEA ©2020

Cataloguing in Publishing Data
Title: Becoming a Daughter of the King
Author: Sharon Reynolds
Subjects: Personal memoir, Christian life, Spirituality

I dedicate this book to my Heavenly Father,
my earthly father, my loving husband, my beautiful children,
and to all those who have stood with me in the battlefield for freedom.

To my best friend — Thank you, Holy Spirit.

FOREWORD

Every woman has a story to tell, but many hide their stories in shame only allowing others to view the perfect pieces. Sharon Reynolds has artfully illustrated her less than perfect journey, but in an amazingly beautiful way. You can relate to what she has penned down for you. You'll find pieces of yourself in her story, and you too will experience healing such as she has. Read her book first by yourself, and then with a friend. It's an encounter from beginning to end.

Jennifer Eivaz

Executive Pastor, Harvest Church Turlock, CA, USA

Founder, Harvest Ministries International

PREFACE

My story is one of radical encounters, incredible adventures and sometimes bizarre timeframes, but I can assure you right from the start that everything you are about to read is true!

What does it mean to become a Daughter of The King? For me, it has meant a process of transformation that has taken place in my life since my first encounter with Jesus Christ in a movie theatre. It is a process that has taken me from a place of ruin into a place of acceptance, a journey of growing in assurance that I am worthy of love and that I am loved by my Father, the Almighty God, the one who has given me peace, both in in this life, and for eternity. He is the one who raised my head between his gentle hands, causing me to look beyond my circumstances and to understand that I am His child now and forever.

I was raised in Upper Hutt, a small town in the North Island of New Zealand about an hour's drive from the capital, Wellington. I felt I had a fairly ordinary upbringing; it wasn't until writing this book, in fact, that I began to see how extraordinary my life has actually been, and how God has always been leading and guiding me towards this understanding that I truly am His Daughter, a Daughter of the King.

We were a small family; I had two parents and one brother, but my parents had many friends who we considered part of our larger, extended 'family.' My parents didn't have much contact with their own family members in the early years of my life—they had both been raised in State Care for some years, and so they had a different perspective on what family was. From an early beginning, I adopted that same understanding . . . that family was more than blood-relatives; it was whoever you chose to become family with.

They were an unlikely combination. My mother was of Maori descent, and my father was European, but they were good people at heart and did the best with what they had as young parents still in their twenties, to raise my brother and me. They had little, but they worked hard . . . and they partied hard with what they had!

For most of my younger years we lived in 'state housing' properties alongside other working-class families. It was only when I started college that we moved into a nicer area and my parents purchased their first and only home. This became our family home for the rest of our growing up years, and my parents remained in that house until my father passed away and my mother downsized to a retirement unit.

I had no experience of anything religious as I grew up, other than knowing that both my parents were 'non-practicing Catholics' and that occasionally we were required to attend weddings, christenings and funeral services—which, from my childish perspective, involved a lot of standing up, kneeling down, and sitting on hard wooden pews. There was nothing that particularly drew me to those church services, but I did enjoy the beautiful architecture and on occasion would go into the church at the end of my street purely to enjoy the solitude and take in the aged atmosphere. I felt at peace whenever I was in these places, but I had no idea why. My mother found this odd, calling me 'Mother

Superior' in her teasing way, but she didn't really mind—to her, church seemed like a safer place for me to hang around than many others.

We were brought up in a very social atmosphere of drinking and late-night parties, and there was always a celebration or two to be had. I became an expert at the board game Monopoly from a young age, often playing into the wee hours of those parties with the kids who had come with their parents. Babysitters in those days were for people with money to spare—at our parties, the kids just got put in one room together and left there until the adults were done.

I was a bit awkward-looking as a kid, with thick, bushy hair that was very hard to tame, and glasses that took over most of my face. I wasn't very good at sport, but I was an avid reader and would often curl up with a good book and get lost for hours, especially if it was a good Enid Blyton adventure. My father encouraged this and was an avid reader and, being a lover of books himself, would often find the money for me to order the next novel in a series from The Lucky Book Club at school. Education and knowledge were important to him and he instilled this in me also.

I found it easy to dive into the fantastical worlds that books created. They became a place of escapism for me, but also began to activate within me the ability to 'see' into other worlds using my imagination. This would be when I would say that the 'Seer' gift began to surface in my life. I didn't recognize it until my adult years, and it took a long time before I would understand it fully. I would often be labelled a 'dreamer,' but my dreaming was very real to me.

To put it simply, a Seer is able to 'see' into spiritual atmospheres; he or she can see into other realms and dimensions, either visually or through visions, dreams or impressions. This is a prophetic gifting, and it comes with great responsibility—learning how it is carried and released requires development and maturity. At the same time, it can be a very difficult calling to navigate.

From an early age I sensed there was more to life than my current surroundings offered. I had a hunger to do better and live better, which drove me to work hard and achieve good results at school. Then, just before I started college, my parents sent me away to a week-long camp at El Rancho in Waikanae, about an hour from our home. There, for the first time, I heard about Jesus Christ and was given a Good News Bible. For a few weeks after that camp, I received encouraging devotions and crossword puzzles in the mail, but once they stopped coming my interest was no longer there.

My mother loves to tell people even to this day how for a time after the camp I pursued God and went on my own to almost every church in our small town, but that nothing ever stuck. I guess it was a bit random and odd for a twelve-year-old in those days to go to church alone. I don't think anyone knew what to make of it, and even I had no explanation for why I was really attending, other than that I was looking for 'something.' Still, it wasn't long before the camp and the importance of my pursuit became a distant memory.

At age thirteen, as I embarked on my college years and my looks were transformed, I blossomed into an attractive young lady. Having crossed the threshold of teenage awkwardness, I quickly became overconfident—my mouth began to take over, and with my newfound attitude it began to get me into trouble; it never disappointed on delivering, and I managed to get burnt often. Over time, my promising grades started to slip, along with my interest in academic achievements.

In my sixth form year I was drawn into an early sexual encounter. That, combined with the drinking culture among my new group of friends, was all it took—I gave up pursuing academic achievements. My father, however, required that if I was going to drop out of achieving my University Entrance qualification, I must either find employment or stay at school. Quickly, I started the application and interview process and managed to wing it enough to gain a fulltime job working as a Junior Claims Assessor. This new freedom of becoming a 'working adult' came with wages that were, after paying a small amount of board, mine to spend in whatever way I wished.

As I had grown, however, so had my parents. They were now in their thirties; their attitudes and values had changed—along with their expectations for my behavior. I, on the other hand, had become quite rebellious, and it was when I began to display a disregard for the sanctuary of our home, that my father began to lay down ultimatums. Shortly before my sixteenth birthday, after an argument with my father, I left home in a defiant act, with nothing but my suitcase in hand.

Lacking the maturity for such a move, it was not long before a succession of big-mouthed events soon required my family to rescue me from one flat after the other. Eventually, I landed myself in hospital, having tried to take my own life. Having had my stomach pumped—and feeling very sorry for myself in my failed attempt—it didn't take much, in my vulnerable state, for a visiting Romeo to sweep me off my feet.

Needing somewhere to recover without drama or conflict after the suicide attempt, I moved in with some older friends who had a spare room to offer. My family knew nothing of my hospitalization, though they were concerned for me. At age eighteen, however, I had already lived without supervising adults for several years. Now, the offer to come and live with my newfound romantic interest was too tempting, and off I ran into his arms without a clue who he really was.

This set me upon the road of my own undoing. Years of hurt-filled relationships followed one after the other. From the age of eighteen to thirty-two, my life was lost to lies, deceit, pain and one stupid decision after the other. During that time, I gave birth to two girls who grew, despite my poor efforts at mothering, into kind, caring and capable young women. Although my family stayed in touch, I put on a good face at least once a year at Christmas; as a result, they never really knew what my life had become.

My journey to becoming a 'Daughter of the King' began in a similar way to my downfall. Bad relationships had pulled me off-track. It was also a relationship—more wonderful than I could ever have imagined—that restored me to a path to life and dignity and hope. That journey began when I met Jesus.

I share this story as a source of inspiration and encouragement to anyone who finds themselves in a place of despair. May my story bring hope to your situation, deliver you from darkness and bring you into the light that is waiting for you.

1

DESPERATION

Waking one morning to yet another round of my neighbors' senseless fighting on their front lawn, I looked out from my lounge window feeling such dissatisfaction with where I had ended up and what life had become. I was thirty-two years old, a single mother of two girls, struggling to make sense of the world I had established for myself. My future had once been bright, yet somehow it had all turned around, and now I was nowhere, doing nothing, feeling life pass me by. The insignificance and poverty were not what I had imagined for my life. I was desperate to find a way out of it all.

Suddenly, I sensed that life had more to offer than what was on display through my window that morning. I wanted to be hopeful despite my circumstances. Somewhere deep within me were the dreams of my youth. I was disappointed in myself for not achieving the academic success I should have and for dropping out of school instead. I felt I had deeply disappointed my father, whose unspoken expectation was that I would rise above the life I had been born into. Instead, with not one child now but two, and still no husband, I seemed destined to be stuck living in State Housing rental houses forever.

That particular day, however, something in me shifted. Rather than make friends with the grief and slip into another round of depression over my circumstances, the warrior within began to rise out of my dissatisfaction. A surge of energy poured through me, and as I yelled through the window to my neighbors, 'Shut up!' for the third time that week, I began to get motivated about making changes. I had the power within me to make things different! I knew what to do! After all, I had plenty of ideas swimming inside of me—all I needed was to get them in order. Or so I thought.

I began to develop a list. 'From here on, *no more losers!*' I wrote. That needed to be *top* of my list, I decided, because my judgement when it came to men had been severely lacking over the years, and the desire for their acceptance had come with a heavy price to pay.

The list began to flow from within me as all the material things I wanted in life made their way onto the paper. In reality though, the thing I was most longing for, at the top of my list, was love. I didn't want to make any further compromises, even if they looked like *love,* yet again! But inside, I was wrestling.

Hindsight is such a gift, and in looking back I can see very clearly that what I thought was love at that time was nothing compared to the true love I would one day find. Whilst seeking companionship and acceptance from the world around me, what I had done in trying to understand myself was to place my worth into another's hands. It was one of the many mistakes that I would keep on repeating over the years—though it looked different in different relationships, it was always the same.

When self-worth is diminished by rejection on any level, it gives root to the opposite of love and something grows from there. My life choices had left me broken hearted and lacking a healthy self-image. People around me thought I was confident yet within my heart bitterness had taken up residence, I felt abandoned, I was self-destructing in every way, and any direction of moral compass had already left the building! The cracks in my soul began to get wider as I found myself continuously experiencing rejection in relationships. Somehow, I had begun to believe the lie that I was a person of far lesser value in my own eyes and those of my society.

I was trying to embrace the dreams hidden deep within me, yet as a single mother I was faced with the constant practical needs right in front of me. As a result, my list became more focused on possessions and things I imagined would bring me happiness. The need for deliverance from my perceived poverty was driving me, but what kept working its way back to the top of my list was the intense desire for a loving relationship — someone who would be good to me and take care of me, someone who would love me and my children as their own, someone who could offer me relief from this financial bind I felt I was in.

My focus was so 'off,' but this was what consumed my mind continuously, it had such a grip on me in every way. Life had taken enough turns, and as a thirtyish-year-old mother, I felt I could never save enough for a deposit on a house, never mind all the expenses that come with owning a home. Despite all of that, however, I genuinely believed that the girls and I needed the stability that a home offered. Amongst all my fanciful dreaming was the reality that what I needed most of all was someone who could provide enough income so that I could buy a house of my own!

Renting was a nightmare. My girls and I were surrounded by a constant stream of fighting families, drug users, dealers—and the continuous theme of a poverty mindset which was always there, bringing me down. Soon, the priority of having a home of my own silenced my romantic notions and, like a voice of reason, it boomed at me—'*Stop dreaming and start living in the real world!*'

But the thought of doing better in life on my own felt impossible. My morals had already sunk to rock bottom, and so, when I was fueled by friendly encouragement to enter the '*realm of the internet,*' it seemed an easy choice. My friend had discovered online dating and assured me that the benefits of wealthy, lonely men outweighed my reality, and so, grabbing the lifeline to another world that proposed endless possibilities, we hatched a plan to entice our future husbands together. At least this way, I thought, I wouldn't have to meet anyone in person—I could work my magic from the keyboard! I had found a quick solution to all my problems, one that required little effort on my part.

By now, thinking I had lost my soul and become secretly devoid of any moral compass my youth had provided, I presumed it would be of no real consequence to take that loss to a whole new level and exchange it for the future I so desired. Essentially, what I was about to do was nothing less than selling myself for the end goal of what I believed would bring me security. I didn't see it like that at the time of course, but in the harsh light of self-reflection further down the road I had to face up to the truth that that is exactly what took place.

Thankfully, the woman I am today is in no way a reflection of the woman I was then.

Unspoken covenants with an unseen enemy are so easily made, and often we do not understand how our emotionally-driven decisions can lead us into the very depths of hell. Hell has many looks and it is not always fire and brimstone. Sometimes it is a prison inside your own mind.

My experience of a life I believed to be unworthy of a 'Daughter of a King' had left me in a pit of anxious misery, gripped by the graveclothes of death, and moving in all the wrong directions. Online dating was just another one of those seemingly dumb decisions that I thought would have no real consequence. What I now know is that nothing truly happens in isolation—there are always consequences, whether they are natural or eternal.

Online dating and computers were a comparatively new phenomenon at the time; in my sphere, not even a handful of people had computers, never mind knew how to use them properly. But I soon got 'the bug' for the online world—it provided a place of comfort and warmed my ego daily.

Eventually I managed to scrape together enough money to buy my own computer. Now I could go online in the privacy of my home rather than spending countless hours looking over my friends' shoulder waiting my turn.

I had no idea what I was doing most of the time but managed to find 'new friends' in an online community who were overjoyed at the prospect of coaching me. Spending countless hours online through the day and then into the night hours as I crossed international time zones, I found plenty of willing participants to assist me in my search for love.

During an evening of online mischief (and admittedly, several glasses of cheap wine), I set up an online dating account and got bold and sassy with my requirements of the 'perfect' mate. With nothing to lose and plenty of distance in-between, I had gained confidence by my interactions in online, international forums. Now I was ready to put my plan into action by stepping into a local forum. From there, all I needed to do was to bravely bring the virtual love world into my reality.

This new sense of self gave me a boldness beyond myself as I began to type in my 'alter-ego' description, and my 'minimum standards': *'Must have a Gold Card and salary of $50,000 or more* (which back then felt like a huge amount of money!), and *'No previous convictions, no ex-anybody hanging around in the background, and no children!'* It was selfish I know, but by now I was operating under a very misguided, inflated sense of self-importance created from my online status. My risen warrior within was beyond tolerating anything less than what was going to get me ahead. 'With my parameters set so ridiculously high, tough and ruthless,' I reasoned, 'surely anyone who responded would have to be worthy of my consideration.'

I thought that being intentionally cut-throat in my demands would weed out potential 'losers.' Besides, I didn't think it likely anyone would really respond to what was being served up, since it probably read more like a dish of 'rudeness, demands and greed' with a side salad of 'slightly nasty and cold.' Nevertheless, the challenge had been thrown down, and the label 'gold-digger' fitted my persona perfectly!

The morning after my advert went live, I lay in bed nursing a rather well-deserved headache from the previous evenings' drunken escapades, but rather than lying in a place of self-pity I decide to get up. My feet buckled slightly under the truth of my sad state as they hit the ground. Full of regret I wandered towards my computer, ready to delete my profile with all its narcissistic demands. And then, I noticed my email icon was flashing wildly. As I opened my mailbox, a flurry of replies to my sassy advert flooded my screen like a raging flood of emails that had burst from their dam after being held up overnight! My inbox was literally overflowing with waiting heartbeats that had responded to my online presence. 'Well, that was completely unexpected!' I laughed to myself. Oh, my goodness! What had I done?

Nursing my pounding head, I turned away from the computer astounded, and lay back down allowing the reality of what was happening to roll over me. Like a Ferrari speeding down a disappearing roadway, I wanted to jump in and respond. On one hand, I was super excited to open all the responses, but I knew a moment of calm reflection was required before the onslaught. I proceeded to wade through the replies and had a great time casting aside those who looked or sounded less than hopeful. It really was a cutthroat exercise, but one that produced a lot of laughter at others expense. 'It's okay,' I told myself. 'They're never going to know, right?'

I occasionally remember that day and it leaves me pondering how much my life changed from that point on, how in an instant the most simplistic actions can bring about such life changing events. Like the Samaritan woman in John 4, whose empty pot and need for water were metaphors for her empty life, my life too was empty. My pot was desperate to be filled, just like hers.

Although her actual name (Photine) is relatively unknown to this day, 'the woman at the well' is as well-known as the need to be loved that she represents. This woman, who came to her local well in search of water for the thirst of herself and her household, was of no importance in her community at all. In fact, just like me, she was someone her community preferred not to see. This is why she is found skulking in the midst of the day, dipping in and out of the shadows cast from the heat of the baking sun while the rest of her town lay resting in shade after sharing a hearty midday meal. Picking up her large clay pot, she purposefully locates the town well, knowing that at this hour there will be no accusing eyes following her every step or whispering voices in the shadows as she passes by.

But when she arrives at the well, she encounters a man—Jesus of Nazareth, a Jew. That day, Jesus had left Judea to journey toward Galilee, but along the way, God redirected him to the small town of Sychar. And since this was not the most direct route to where he was heading, there must have been a reason for taking this seemingly 'long way' around.

As it turns out, this was no insignificant stop along the way for Jesus. What he was about to find in Sychar was a woman with a great need, because, her loneliness had not gone unnoticed by God and so he sent Jesus, very specifically, to meet this one woman.

From her side, it was out of her cultural norm to interact with a Jew, lest of all a Jewish man. But as the true love of God in him reached out and touched the need in her, she found herself reacting in a new and culturally unexpected way, engaging him in conversation regardless of all the reasons why she shouldn't!

Jesus then calls her out, exposing her sin and her need, but he does so in such love that it doesn't sting at all. The void of loneliness she's been trying to mask with one relationship after the other is identified by this complete stranger, and finally she responds with a plea, asking to be filled with the water he offers.

Like the woman at the well, I too had been in many relationships—none of them good—and still I had no husband. I had escaped to the shelter of a women's refuge with my first child still in the womb, and now the shame of having two children to two different fathers had left me socially distant. Just like her, the awareness of people looking down on me caused me to skulk in the shadows of my community. My need was as great as hers, yet isolation, not hope, had become my comforter. My pot was similar to hers too. I could identify with the hopelessness and the need; my loneliness was equal in its desire to be relieved. But where was *my* Savior, *my* knight in shining armor, *my* rescuer and redeemer—where was *that* guy? Why had he not come for me?!

Well, it was simple really. I had missed the moment . . . several of them, actually! Just like the 'woman at the well,' I had no knowledge that God was even looking out for me, nor did I realize at the time that He had already come for me on more than one occasion in my lifetime. He had knocked quite loudly at times, it turned out, but I had chosen repeatedly to ignore the invitation. Unlike the woman at the well who left her need behind, here I was still holding mine so tightly. Like a heavy clay pot, my need was weighing me down, yet I clutched it even tighter.

The Samaritan woman's need was what brought her to the well that day, but after an encounter with this unforgettable man her life changed dramatically in a single moment. She went from obscurity and lack of reputation to becoming reputable and known overnight, transformed from need to glory, and a whole society was freed in the process. From this meeting, she went on to spread the good news of this true love throughout her nation. She became the first woman evangelist in history!

What I would reflect back on and realize in the years to come, was how closely my story and the Samaritan woman's aligned. Yet she chose Jesus in her moment of anguish, and I still had not. My time was running out. The opportunities for change were diminishing daily. But thank God, He never gives up. My moment of choice was about to come, yet again. There was still hope for me.

It seems silly that I would turn once again towards men for my salvation, but that's exactly what I did. Some people are slow at learning from their pain, and I was definitely one of them! That morning, as I sifted through the cascading flow of emails, I hoped that at least one of them had the answer I so badly needed.

Inside each of us lies a desire to be needed and loved—as I read through the sheer volume of email responses, my heart was touched by the desperation others shared to simply love and be loved in return. All it took was a few emails back and forth and a couple of mismatched blind dates, before I discovered a man who wanted love just as much as I did, someone who longed for me to meet his craving for affection.

Who in their wildest dreams would have thought that a brash moment online would find me in the grip of such love?! The prayers I never prayed had been answered at last! Somehow, the universe in its infinite wisdom had taken my garbled, self-promoting words, born out of drunken frustration, and dressed them in such a way that they had landed upon the right heart, a *good* heart!

Hearts have such a large responsibility. They courageously carry the capacity for life and death to the entire body, yet they can be so easily crushed and broken. *'A good heart is hard to find . . .'* How true those words had become for me.

My own *'good heart'* had already experienced temporary love and much grief because of it. Now a crust had begun to form over my heart and, much like the roughness of the outside of a *Paua* shell, it was going to take a whole lot of grinding to get my heart to shine with the beauty it was created for. But just like the beautiful colors inside the *Paua* shell, the beauty was there.

My short-lived attempt at becoming a 'gold-digger' had turned up a man who on the outside ticked most of the boxes on my list. Despite his unkempt outward appearance and ever-present alcoholism, I was sure I could manage this relationship to my own advantage and keep my heart from further damage. Despite my wrong motives, I believed I could navigate the obvious discrepancies, and was ready to make the necessary compromises required to meet the goals on my list (remember that list!).

The man who had found me online was so lovingly devoted toward me that it blinded my heart to all the sensible reasons why this relationship might not work. He could see the good in me and regardless of the obstacles, I could see his goodness too, deep within. I was still so far from God, unaware that he was drawing me to himself. Without either of us realizing it at the time, God had brought us together for His purposes—purposes which were yet to unfold.

> *'I have loved you with an everlasting love;*
> *therefore I have drawn you with loving devotion.'*
> Jeremiah 31:3

On the surface it felt as if all that had gone wrong in life was now coming right. I was at ease, assured that the goodness I had planned for my life would now be fulfilled. Since meeting each other, a lot of changes had taken place in rapid succession. We quickly settled into my rental home together and both moved into new jobs—I was now a careers guidance counsellor with a private training establishment, and Craig transitioned from working in a government helpdesk position to supervising a small team as an I.T. engineer at a local hospital. And, despite all the changes and the difficulties that becoming a 'blended' family can often bring, our girls adapted well from a one parent family to a two-parent family and welcomed Craig into their lives with open arms.

It was a huge risk and maybe a little impulsive, but when the proposal came less than a year later, I was willing to take the gamble. Even though we had only known each other a short time, I said 'yes!'—and with that, the list of my desires I had created for my future and that of my family seemed suddenly possible. With our combined incomes we were able to pay for a wedding and save for a deposit on our first home. Finally, the security my heart had so desperately desired would be resolved.

Our wedding was a joyous occasion. My wishes had come true! I had found a good man who, it seemed, idolized me and loved my daughters as if they were his own. All the scars of the years of betrayal and loneliness from bad relationships and poor decisions melted away. What more could I possibly want!? We were married. We'd formed a new family, and everyone was happy.

That is, until the wheels began to fall off our 'perfect compromise.'

2

THE JOURNEY BEGINS

When I got married, I thought long and hard about what it would mean for me in terms of my identity. Over time I had built relationships within my community, through my work as guidance counsellor, and in the networks I had established as a result of the various workplace contracts I had taken since having the girls. My last name, known to many in my community from my family's longstanding involvement at the local tavern helped considerably when I referred clients for job positions . . . why would I change it?

In those days, it was quite a modern idea for women to keep their maiden names, or to hyphenate their surname, and I wanted to be a modern woman. However, there were also advantages to a name change—this was a chance to recreate myself, step into a new identity and leave my past well behind me. With my new persona, I could be free of the shame and guilt of being a single mother with two children to two different fathers. If I took Craig's last name, people would just assume we were—and always had been—one family, and I would never need to explain myself again. Besides, 'Mrs. Reynolds' had a nice ring to it.

And so, I decided to take on a new surname—and with it, everything that went with being a 'Mrs.' only I had no idea what that really meant. For a while I struggled. I had become accustomed to independent living; now I had another person present in all my decisions.

The first thing I discovered that being married did not mean that I had a live-in babysitter. In fact, my new companion found all my comings and goings tiresome, and soon the pressure was on to 'make a home,' as expectations emerged from his upbringing about which I really had no idea at all. My selfish plan, remember, had been to achieve a lifestyle—I had never genuinely wanted to engage deeply with this man.

By now, both of us were in new work situations, and I was taking on increasing amounts of responsibilities as the company I worked for began to restructure and provide more training programs. This gave me the opportunity to step up and take on more of a leadership role; before long I had my own office and was overseeing a team. Things were looking good on that front; I was being groomed to move into more of a management role as the company grew.

Craig's new position also required a lot more commitment, and as his hours and the pressure increased, so did his drinking tendencies and his attitude towards my lack of availability. My idea of the modern wife dressed in power suits and climbing the corporate ladder did not sit well with my husband, whose expectations were more of the 'pipe and slippers brigade;' being served a well-cooked meal every evening and a packed lunch daily was a better objective in his world. Unsurprisingly, conflict began to show its ugly head—while he hid from it, I was in 'full-engage' mode!

It was soon evident that my 'compromise for security' had come with a cost, and I was now wavering in my decision about whether I wanted to pay that price. Rebellious in nature, the idea of domestic enslavement did not sit well with me—I had no inclination to 'serve' this man when I had a household to run, children to raise and a career of my own that was opening up and heading places. As far as I was concerned, he was required to partner with me in all things, and that included domestic chores. I was going to give him the orders when he got home and nip this thing in the bud immediately!

'Who can find a virtuous wife? For her
worth is far above rubies.'
Proverbs 31:10

The dictionary meaning for the word *'virtuous'* is: *having or showing high moral standards*, my standards were already off-balance in this relationship, if only because of my motives for being in it in the first place.

I had been married to my 'good man' for about a year by now, but my unscrupulous sense of survival told me that I needed to sustain at least two years of marriage before I could walk away with enough money in my pocket to realize my list of goals for home ownership and security for my little family that had got me here in the first place. Although we had already bought a home together, my ultimate aim was still to own 'my own home'—in my mind, I never really expected the marriage to last any longer than I needed it too.

It seemed that, in my husband's eyes, the polish had started to come off my worth too, and when I approached him with my dissatisfaction, he did not care much at all for my outburst. This response took me completely by surprise. He had worshipped the ground I walked on, been madly in love and responsive to my every directive. He had idolized me! Now it was as if he had woken from the slumber of infatuation and no longer desired to be so subservient. The bear had come out of hibernation, and what was always lurking behind that 'good heart' began to surface.

The heart of her husband safely trusts her; so he will have no lack of
gain. She does him good and not evil all the days of her life.
Proverbs 31:11-12

Well, that statement could not have been further from the truth in that moment! We had started out simply avoiding each other, but soon the decline of our relationship and the pressure to make it work began to press in from all sides. The truth of my agenda was creeping forward like a snake crawling out from its hidden space into the light of day. All was about to be exposed!

It is amazing to me how, when God gets involved in bringing His love forth into your life, the dark things suddenly find their way into the light and the truth can no longer be hidden like it once was.

To be loved is not the same as loving, and when there is a lack of balance, the scales will begin to tip. We were only a year in, and the honeymoon was certainly over! The excitement of everything being new had gone, and the practical elements of daily living quickly revealed the gaps between us. Now we were struggling with the pressures of being a 'blended family.'

The book of Job talks about one good man and how his life was devastated by painful loss and ruin, and though, unlike Job, I deserved all that was coming to me for my lack of goodness, God had a different plan. Although I did not know it yet, he had already forgiven me, and now I was about to discover *true* goodness for the first time ever.

The story of Job is full of miscommunications and lack of understanding, mixed with the faithfulness of God who, in the end, restores more than what was lost. But it is not a story for the fainthearted. Before everything is set right, Job encounters an incredible amount of destruction. At times, his heart is stretched beyond human capacity. However, the truest love of all gets him through; in the end he is a richer man for it in every aspect of his life and he is recreated in greater glory than before all his troubles began. I didn't know it at the time, but my own story, which resonated so strongly with Job in his sense of loss, was about to turn around too. Like him, I was about to experience the restoration of all that I had lost.

It was only when Craig was gone for a few days to attend a training seminar, that I found some breathing space in the midst of the unfolding calamity. During those few days, the truest love I would ever come to know arrived and changed our lives for eternity.

While Craig was away, a friend invited me to join her for an evening at the movies. *The Passion of the Christ* was screening and knowing that I was an avid film buff, she thought I would enjoy a night out. She was right—an evening out sounded like the perfect distraction from all the troubles and concerns that were bothering me.

I had no idea, however, that this movie was hardly the sort of 'chick flick' we usually would attend! It was actually an intense portrayal of the story of Christ going to the cross. This took me by total surprise! With my mind firmly stuck in my own dilemma, and thoughts of how I was going to survive my marriage long enough to make something from it, I had not taken note of the film reviews or the hype around this movie at the time. And so, blissfully unaware of what I was really attending, off I went for a nice evening out at the movies with a friend.

Soon, however, I found myself locked in as the story unfolded before me and the reality of it began to strike a chord in my heart. I flinched my way through one scene, where the Roman guards arrested Jesus then scourged and beat him, cupping my hands to my face as I watched them mock him, dress him in false robes and label him, 'King of the Jews.' Then suddenly, as I saw a crown of brier thorns being placed upon his head and pushed down into position, an intense flash of indescribable pain rushed through my body! I felt it for less than half a second, I'm certain; had it been any longer, I would surely have passed out. The pain I felt was beyond human measure. I did not know what to do. What had just happened?!

I was frozen in the moment, but as my eyes widened, I looked at the screen and witnessed Christ pick up and carry His cross up the steep incline towards his impending death. A thought crossed my mind — *'This man is not just any man; this man truly is the Son of God!'* The thought came to my mind almost as quickly as the flash of pain had come, but it came directly from my heart, and somehow, I knew it to be true!

I sat silently through the rest of the movie, my gaze transfixed as tears filled my eyes with excruciating grief at what I was witnessing. There was no way any man could possibly have endured all that Christ went through, and then get up and walk the vertical path towards Golgotha, enduring the jeering and mocking of the crowds along the way even though he was completely innocent of any crime. No man could bear the humiliation and pain of the guards continuously whipping him all the way, never mind the weight of the large rough-cut wooden cross hurled upon his beaten shoulders. It was surely impossible for any normal person to survive that amount of physical torture and keep going! What mere man would carry his cross so willingly, knowing his impending death was waiting and that even in dying there was yet more to come?

My heart was flooded with compassion, tears fell from my eyes and love bore a hole in the hardness of my heart as I accepted the truth into my spirit, knowing that this man was God and that He had allowed his own suffering so that I could live. How I knew it, I can't explain. I just did!

Faith is 'the substance of things unseen but hoped for,' and the gift of faith is the ability to remain hopeful and believe even when things look impossible. I received both that night, and I remain forever grateful for those sincere gifts from God.

When the movie came to an end, the whole theatre remained seated. An eerie silence filled the atmosphere. No one moved an inch. I couldn't move either. I didn't know what to do or say next. I just remained stuck in my seat in absolute awe along with the deafening silence and reverence that was holding everyone else in place too.

Eventually the crowd began to disperse out of the theatre, slowly and quietly, one by one. As the somber mood lifted a little, I was able to pluck myself from my seat too, wondering silently to myself what was going on inside of me. I thanked my friend and excused myself from joining her for a late-night drink, then ran for the safety of the carpark where I locked myself in my car as a river of tears gushed forward. As I drove home, all I could think was, 'What has just happened, what does it mean, and why did I feel that in such a real way?' I had no answers, but I needed them.

When I arrived home, I picked up a Bible the kids had been given by the same friend who had taken me to the movie that night, and upon opening it I found these words from John 3:16 inside the cover: '*For God loved the world so much that he gave his only Son, so that everyone who believes in him may not die but have eternal life.*'

The verse was followed by a statement of welcome into the family of God; and it said that for those who had made this choice, there was still more . . . that if you believed, you could also receive the Holy Spirit! One thing was sure—I was not one to hold back from gaining a full measure of anything, So, I read on. As I lay down on my bed that night and followed the prayer in the book, I asked God to forgive me for all my sins and thanked Him for Jesus Christ, who I now knew to be the Son of God. I asked Him to fill me with His Spirit—and as I did, suddenly what seemed like a light rush of wind entered my room and swiftly lifted me upwards off the bed a centimeter or so!

It is hard to describe the sensation, and unless you have experienced it personally, I not sure that my words could give justice to the experience, other than to say that it was like a giant *whoosh* went through me and I was softly laid back down. In that moment, I felt my heart fill with something I had never been aware of before. It was love, true love, the sort of love I would come to know as *agape* love (God's love) in the days and years ahead.

God's love is not like that of human love, it is unconditional and beyond measure, the fullness and completeness of all He is . . . and then it's in you! I had complete and total peace in that moment, and I quickly drifted off to sleep.

The gift of faith I was given that day was extraordinary. All I can tell you is that my encounter with Jesus was so real that I have never been able to deny it (or Him!) from that moment on. In fact, I believe that because of the intensity of my encounter with Christ, the gift of faith that I received has made me unmovable, not only in my belief that Jesus is real, but that whatever the Bible says he could do, I can too!

I have come to learn throughout my journey with Jesus that not everyone has such a radical moment of encounter. And so, while I thought that perhaps I just had a usual measure of faith, I now realize that I have indeed been given an incredible gift of faith—I truly had supernatural ability to simply believe, without question!

The next morning, when I woke full of joy, I knew that life was never going to be the same again. I normally hated washing the dishes, but that morning as I washed the dishes, I found myself singing! It was like the moment in 'Snow White and the Seven Dwarfs' where Snow White flings open the wooden shutters and little birds start singing along with her as she scrubs heartily at the sink! The transformation was noticeable alright—even the kids could see that something was up, and it was something beyond *just good*! Something had changed overnight. Just like the Samaritan woman, I had met a man that had changed my life in an instant. Now I felt compelled to tell anyone who would listen . . . and even many who would not!

The most pressing issue however, was, *what on earth was I going to tell my husband?* He was due home later that day and the woman he had left behind was no longer there! What he was about to find was not at all what he was expecting. My heart began to panic with dread and fear. I was out of my depth with this and there was no immediate help in sight, so I turned to the only one I could and for the first time in my life prayed purposefully to the God I now acknowledged. 'God, please give me the right words to say,' I prayed. 'Help me to keep my life and not lose everything just because I chose you.'

It was a self-focused prayer and I was so very raw emotionally, but I knew for the first time in so long that I was completely and wholly loved. Surrounded in God's love, I sensed everything was going to be okay, and although I couldn't totally relax, I was no longer afraid of losing anything. He was going to take care of me! I had *faith*!

Therefore, if anyone is in Christ, he is a new creation; old things have passed away; behold, all things have become new.
2 Corinthians 5:17

I might have been a new creation, but the reality of my latest life decision was about to come home to roost as my husband walked through the door. He threw his jacket loosely over the chair next to me in a less than sober manner. 'Some things are better left for the cold light of a new day,' I thought to myself momentarily. How could I even begin to explain that in an instant my whole being had experienced a supernatural event that had transformed me from years of living one way to suddenly wanting to pursue a complete opposite direction? It was all beyond reason, and to now articulate this news to someone who was deeply rooted in logic and possessed greater knowledge and understanding of things than I did, presented as an impossible task.

Not heeding the thought of waiting until morning, I launched into telling Craig my story that very evening — and in that moment, the seed from my childhood began to spring forth and the seer gift within me was activated under the creative power of the Holy Spirit that now resided within me. I had always been a pretty good liar, but this was a different creative energy I was experiencing — as I called my husband to come and sit with me in our front room, the words just began to flow from the very heart of God and out of my mouth. I was as surprised to speak them as he was to hear them!

I shared with Craig about the movie and the transformation that had taken place in me overnight, as he sat, patiently listening. 'I had a dream last night,' I told him, 'where the Holy Spirit showed me that within a year, if we continue living the way we have been, we won't be married much longer, and in the process each of us will become casualties and so wounded in our hearts that we may never recover from the hurt.' I explained that God had shown me that, rather than opting for a short-lived two years of marriage, there was another alternative before us. Another pathway was being offered and we were standing at a crossroad and had choices to make.

I began to express this to my husband with all my heart, and as I did so, a vision opened up in front of me and I spoke out what I could see: Jesus had stood in my place in front of an oncoming truck that just couldn't be stopped. Christ had happily plucked me from its path and took my place, knowing He would die so that I could live. There was no greater love than to lay down your life for another, and He had done this so willingly! *Would Craig do the same for me?* It was like seeing a movie reel play out in front of me, but I was speaking every detail as I saw it, and at the same time trying to keep my composure to relate what I could see without completely freaking out myself as it happened!

I wanted my husband to have what I had found. With all my being I longed for his heart to be touched and transformed in the same way as mine. I knew he was a man with a good heart underneath the overwhelming smell of alcohol and tobacco, but I also discerned deep down that the dream about our marriage and the oncoming truck was also accurate. And so, as we sat there together, I gave him an ultimatum. 'I feel so strongly about this,' I said, 'and I want us to do this together, but I don't think I can be in a marriage where one believes and the other doesn't.'

I admitted to Craig that I had entered into this marriage with all the wrong motives, and that I regretted it now, but as I told my husband more of the dream and that God had revealed to me that there was a happy future ahead for us, there was no way I was now going to let go of that promise. If there was a mighty future ahead for us, I was prepared to fight for it!

As I spoke, the visions kept coming thick and fast from heaven, and I saw that there was so much more to gain in this true love from God than from any love we had ever known before. I sensed His Presence and felt His love as I poured out my vision—it was overwhelmingly beautiful and rich in pleasure, and I tried so hard to articulate this to my husband in a desperate effort to gain his agreement. In my zeal and excitement of belief, I was essentially asking him to accept Christ as *his*

Savior for the sake of *our* future! All kinds of wrong I know, but hey, that's just how it was on the day! My husband loved and adored me— right? But confronted with this ultimatum, would that be enough?

Craig's initial reaction took me by surprise. He did not completely rebuke me or question my testimony. He didn't reject my revelations, but what I was proposing was a lot to process. I wondered if I had overplayed my hand and gone just a tad too far. Still slightly hung over after arriving home from his business trip, he expressed his reservations about what I'd told him. He needed time to think, he said. Impatient as ever, I pushed him a little further, but although manipulation was one of my stronger tools, when I confronted him with, 'If you love me . . .' the line backfired as he replied, 'Well, I'm not sure I do!'

What? Confusion and panic took over my heart that had, until that moment, been so compassionate and full of peace. *What should I do next?!* But God's ways are not our ways and fighting with my husband or trying to talk him around was not an option; Craig was highly competitive and very stubborn when he thought he might lose. All I could do was trust God. This was going to have to be His fight, as I had no skin in this game at all.

As my husband walked away from our conversation I sat, stunned, on the edge of the bed, tears welling up inside of me as I faced the fear that my world was about to crumble all over again. *Oh Lord, what had I done?*

Craig's Story

When Sharon asked me if I would stand in front of a truck for her like Jesus and take the hit so she may live, I answered with a resounding 'No!' and couldn't understand why she looked so shocked at my answer. Who in their right mind would ever do such a thing?!

My wife had clearly changed, and she wanted me to change with her, and although I wasn't terribly opposed, I also don't like to be pushed into things. I had fallen in love thinking that being married to her would meet my needs, but as she sat in front of me pouring out her heart, I realized that actually, I didn't possess any real love for her at all.

She had just presented me with a demand that seemed to require an immediate response, and all I could think was 'how am I ever going to get out of this mess?' The yearning to run was in me, yet my feet stayed fixed firmly to the floor. When she had spoken, something had been stirred inside me. I was going nowhere, and deep down I knew it!

Like Sharon, I had grown up in a working-class family with two parents and one brother, however my parents were fairly reserved compared to hers and life was rather uneventful. We weren't very social people at all and kept to ourselves mostly; I only ever lived in two houses and went to church with my mother and brother until I reached my teens, when it became too hard for my mother to drag me out of bed on a Sunday. I was a good student and excelled at high school, however, I wasn't prepared for the independence of university and soon realized that I could sit in a bar all day and still be paid my student allowance rather than going to the lectures.

After three years of failing university, I succeeded at working the graveyard shift at a local petrol station. One of my regular customers learned of my computer knowledge and interest and offered me a week's work filling in on a helpdesk for an internet provider. This led to a career in information technology . . . and alcohol abuse.

Despite my lack of self-esteem and drinking habits, Sharon was available, and I wanted a wife and a family, so I married her. Why not, I figured. Some weeks later I found myself in a church service with Sharon and the girls when the Pastor gave a call for prayer. I still didn't even know why I was there really; I just knew that I had to be, but when he gave the invitation, it was as if I was being pulled towards the front and my heart was pounding. Before the pastor began praying, he asked me if I wanted to give my life to Christ. I simply said, 'Yes,' and as he prayed for me, he also prayed for the spirit of alcoholism to leave me. I have not had a drop of alcohol since.

Thus began our new life together of radical faith, signs, miracles and wonders following. But while Sharon's incredible encounter had left her in awe of Jesus and in love with God believing everything He spoke, I took some time to mull over the writings of the Good News Bible I had kept from my childhood. Hers had been a radical transformation to faith and mine, it's fair to say, was to be more like a slow boil.

Craig had confronted his fears and stepped forward to a prayer call that changed his life in an instant. Once the alcoholism left him, so did memories that had been entrenched within the drink. Not all of his memories were erased—he remembers significant moments, like the conversation I had with him in the front room that day about Jesus and being in front of the truck that would ultimately kill me, and he remembers that vividly the ultimatum I gave. He remembers the important things, and I'm glad he doesn't remember the rest. He had gone from being an alcoholic overnight to being completely sober, and this was only the beginning of many miracles we were about to discover on this journey together.

The pastors at our new church took us under their wings to personally disciple us. As an intellectual, Craig had a lot more questions than I did, but once we got past his need for an explanation for everything, our spiritual growth accelerated and our love blossomed as it was meant to have been all along.

Soon we made the decision to get water-baptized. We both agreed this was an important declaration we needed to make publicly as well as privately. At the same time, we decided to renew our wedding vows — this time, with Christ at the center. My first wedding ring had been an open-ended band rather than a closed circle, so my husband bought a new ring to put a seal upon our marriage as an outward demonstration of the covenant relationship we had entered into with God and each other this time around. Not long after, I stood proudly with our two girls as they made their own journey to the baptismal pool and shared their testimonies, before Craig, along with our pastor, lowered them into the water. It was a day of great celebration for us all!

What reassurance I had! Our family was going to be held together by faith, and now that we understood what a marriage 'covenant' truly meant, I knew we would never part. Gods promise had come to pass. We had made our choice, our marriage had been saved, and now it was true love that bound us, rather than the convenience of two people in need of each other. We heard the Lord whispering to us both: *'You have become the word, the living truth of my presence on earth.'*

It was Craig who received revelation about the word God had spoken — that God had breathed His breath of life onto our union and onto us as individuals, and that we now carried heaven within us. We didn't have to wait for heaven to come to earth . . . it was already here, in us! This unique perspective of our new identity in Christ strengthened us in our understanding of who we were as a Son and Daughter of the King. It was a radical perspective, but we knew no different!

We had been recreated in each other's eyes, and for us it meant we needed to create new memories. Our individual pasts, along with our false start of a marriage with all the lies and shame of what it was, had been left behind. We had a fresh start in front of us—a real hope and a real shot at a great future together as a family. Now we were full of promise, and together we could create great memories that would last.

We set about creating a new future and embarked upon our newfound faith as a family together. We were all on a journey, and it felt right to be walking on the same path. Thankfully, the warning God had given me never came to pass; our marriage did not die, Craig and I did not divorce or hurt each other terribly in the process. Instead, the opposite came true in every possible way. As we put what we read into practice we began to experience the incredible signs, wonders and miracles that have now become a staple in our lives.

3

GRACE FOR THE JOURNEY

As we embarked on this new journey together, we soon discovered there was more ahead of us than what laid behind. The transformation process of change is not easy. Watch a caterpillar turning into a butterfly sometime and you will see the pressing and squeezing that goes on inside a chrysalis filled with black goop. It is gruesome, but it yields beautiful results.

Finally, we were walking together, figuring out our newfound love and negotiating the unfamiliar pathways our feet had stumbled upon in the process. When we first married, we had agreed there was no need for more children in our household. I already had two daughters, and a twisted pelvis made bringing life into the world difficult, so it seemed a logical agreement.

On top of that, a few years prior to meeting Craig, I had suffered a mild stroke following a simple operation. Thankfully, I was treated early, and with steroids and physiotherapy, I had made a 95% recovery. The only residual damage was that I started experiencing some flicking in my left eye whenever I became extremely tired or overstressed. I took this as a blessing of sorts—it became my indicator for when I was overdoing things. But the instruction I had been given as I went forward in my recovery was *'no tension, no worries,'* which, as Craig put it, sounded something akin to *'hakuna matata.'* If I could maintain that, I was told, then everything should come right and stay that way. To have more children came with higher risk, and as I was now older, a pregnancy could endanger my health and possibly my life. And since we had no desire for more children at that time anyway, the plan was been made and agreed upon to not pursue adding to our already established family.

Little did we know that, like every other plan we had jointly made, this one was also about to be turned upside down and inside out too!

> *Now faith is the substance of things hoped for,*
> *the evidence of things not seen.*
> Hebrews 11:1

Life really was good for us as we held onto hope and the promises God had given us for our family. We were finding our true selves, falling in love with one another, and growing in so many ways as a family with our new love of Christ. My husband took on the part time role of youth pastor in our church, and soon we had the incredible experience of witnessing God's healing power at work through us!

A young Samoan teenage girl, Sefina (*not her real name*), had not been in New Zealand long when she found her way to our newly-formed youth group. She had only attended twice when we got a call from her parents one evening to tell us their daughter was extremely unwell—she was in the local hospital, and could we please come and pray for her?

When we arrived at the hospital, we soon discovered her situation was much worse than we had first thought. Somehow, she had developed Guillain-Barré syndrome—a rare but serious autoimmune disorder in which the immune system attacks healthy nerve cells in your peripheral nervous system. This leads to weakness, numbness, and tingling, and can eventually cause paralysis. Now Sefina was lying in the Intensive Care Unit, paralyzed and in a coma, breathing through a ventilator. By the time we arrived, the prognosis was that even if she lived through this episode, she could quite possibly never walk again, and if she did it, was going to take lot of intense physiotherapy to get her functioning again.

We could not believe what we were hearing! The family had gathered on the floor of the ICU waiting room and invited us to join in their prayer circle, and although we had no understanding of their language or what was being prayed, we joined in wholeheartedly desiring to see Sefina healed. Feeling the Holy Spirit prompt us to step out in faith and go to her bedside and pray with her directly, and with the family's permission, Craig and I literally stood together, spoke words of life to her, and quietly prayed in tongues as we sat at her bedside and held her hand. We just didn't know what else to do, so we did what we knew.

At some point, a specialist came in and told us that they were going to have to make an incision in the patient's throat in order to create a better airway for her. Boldly, I asked if he could wait until the morning, because, I assured him, she was going to be healed by then, and as a teenage girl, having a scar like that would be very hard for her when she was already struggling with fitting into New Zealand culture. The doctor did not share quite the same resolve that this was going to happen, and went ahead with the plan.

I was so sure of my statement and disappointed in his lack of faith. I just expected others to 'see' like I did, with eyes of faith, but as Craig gently explained, I was unique in that area and others just couldn't see it the same way I did, so it was best not to get upset or frustrated with people. The next day, however, when we went in to visit Sefina, there she was, sitting up as large as life in a lazy-boy hospital chair, talking and smiling!

Later, she told us that while she was in the coma, she could hear us talking and praying for her. She came into agreement with our prayers and asked Jesus into her life, and that night in ICU she was healed. And though she was left with a noticeable scar, within three months she was walking again and singing her heart out in praise to God—she even went on to write a worship song.

Never underestimate what is happening even if you can't see anything! We had no experience, we certainly had flaws, and we weren't religiously trained, but we had faith and we took God at His word and believed it . . . and look what happened!

It was an incredible moment for us all. Then, *surprise!* I became pregnant—and there was double the joy the day we found out I was carrying twins! We were amazed at the gift we had been given. These babies stood for so much in our redemption story. Within such a short period of time everything had changed—our whole lives, our values, our belief systems, everything was different. It seemed that nothing could go wrong.

Until it did.

Just like my previous relationships, my first two pregnancies and deliveries had not been at all smooth. This time, however, I believed it would be different. That was back then—it was the 'old me.' Surely this 'new me' would find this pregnancy easier! Still, I battled against my expectations of a difficult birth and the possibility of another round of post-natal depression, which had been a reality with each birth so far.

Thankfully, this time, I was surrounded by people who freely prayed for me and offered support. One of those was my pastor's wife, who introduced me to an incredible book called 'Supernatural Childbirth.' I had never heard the term before, but as I read, I began to take hold of fresh promises for the months ahead. Already this pregnancy was different in every way to the others, and I was hopeful that none of the past problems would come with it. I was happily married now, this pregnancy was a promise of new life and hope, and I began to relax and believe that all would be well. When we saw our babies for the first time at the twelve-week scan, my concerns and fears faded away, and excitedly we announced the news that we were expecting twins!

Just one week later though, we had to make another, very different, announcement. Our babies had started to form, and our eyes only had just seen them in the scan, but as quickly and unexpectedly as they came, they began to leave, as suddenly one night I began to bleed. 'The substance of the unseen' means those things which our physical sight has yet to lay hold of but are being formed nevertheless—that's faith! Still, in that moment, we rushed to the phone, calling for prayer and babysitters for the girls, then sped down the motorway towards the hospital, trying not to panic, with my husband fiercely declaring God's promises all the way.

The medical team examined me and, finding everything was intact, ordered a night of rest. The next morning, however, when we went in for another scan there was nothing to be seen—no babies, in fact, not even a trace that babies had ever been there. It was as if in the middle of the night we had somehow been robbed and the womb lay empty. I began to wonder if I had seen things or dreamt the whole pregnancy up. Had it not been for my husband at my side I think I could have easily slipped into madness over it because it just made no sense at all.

Our sadness and my impending madness was overridden by incredible grace; I cannot even explain how we got through the next few weeks other than to say we did. There were no more questions for us, we were not hounding heaven for answers, and we had extraordinary peace. Just as easily as they had come, we accepted that our babies had left, and we grieved and kept walking the journey together, hand in hand. The loss of the unseen seems easier than the loss of what is seen, doesn't it—our babies were only thirteen weeks along—and yet when well-meaning people made comments that they were never really here, it didn't help at all.

When you are pregnant you are filled not just with physical flesh and blood as the baby forms, you are filled with hopes, dreams and promises for that child—and you have a part in bringing all of those to fruition. When that hope within you passes, a piece of you goes with it too. For anyone who has lost a child at any stage of pregnancy, I offer the hope that God's grace, which carried me in unspeakable ways, would carry you too. Knowing Jesus and having hope in our lives made our loss so much easier to bear. But what I discounted at the time, was the need to go through the natural process of grieving.

It was some years later that we realized that the experience of losing our babies was compounded by the grief of the years that had gone before. We were unaware we were carrying such unseen pain until one day God spoke to me through another book, unleashing what felt like an endless stream of tears. That night, after I fell asleep, an extraordinary thing happened. The spirit-realms of heaven opened to me. In a dream, God showed me my babies!

In my dream, I saw the most beautiful young man I have ever seen. He was positioned on top of a rock looking beyond a coastline that stretched before him. He had a guitar in his hands, and as he strummed, the most melodic sound came forth—such that has never been heard on earth before, I'm sure! The closer my eyes got, the more he appeared like a typical surfer-type, leather bracelets and everything! There was a soft, gentle, almost angelic-like presence about him. He just radiated absolute beauty. I knew that this was no ordinary boy. My heart instantly adored him and as I stood in awe, a voice simply said, *This is your son, Daniel.'* At that, my heart swelled with love.

My attention was then taken further down the coastline, where I saw a delicate dancer approaching him on the sands. She danced as if on air and her movements were as light as the soft wind that began to blow. She danced as if she were the air itself! The young man's music moved her along, and with every twist and turn as she came nearer, the response between them was both heavenly and glorious to behold. Every step she took was in worship to the Lord, and angels stood admiring her dance as she leapt joyously before them. Again, a voice spoke: *'This is Lydia, your daughter,'* and for the second time my heart overflowed with love as I watched my beautiful children worship and rejoice with the angels who had become their caretakers.

I awoke that night with tears streaming down my face and explained my dream to my husband who marveled at it with me. Craig and I both feel we now know Lydia and Daniel, our children, intimately, and look forward to the day of rejoicing when we will be with them again.

The thief does not come except to steal, and to kill, and to destroy. I have come that they may have life, and that they may have it more abundantly.'
John 10:10

It wasn't long before the promise of new life that had mysteriously evaporated before our eyes was returned to us in abundance when our next two miracle babies arrived close on the heels of each other. With only thirteen months apart, they might as well have been twins!

I say 'miracle babies' because Shaun was discovered during the pregnancy to be feet first and despite efforts to turn him seemed determined to land into this world on his feet standing up! As a result, my natural-birth delivery plan changed, and we were booked to have a caesarean section delivery under general anesthetic. Craig managed to sneak in and be present for the whole thing, which wasn't usually allowed, but he managed to slip into the theatre totally gowned up, and was able to see when the specialist began to remove the baby very delicately because the umbilical cord was wrapped around his neck not only once or twice, but three times. Lucky we had such a good relationship with our specialist! Had I gone into labor, our son Shaun could have been choked and died before he was even born. And so, he truly was a miracle. A healthy baby boy!

It was just over a year later that our daughter, Amy, was born, also via caesarean delivery. This time, however, I was conscious, and Craig was able to keep me company, talking to me through the procedure until our tiny bundle was safely born. At 6 pounds 9 ounces, she was a long baby, but we had to rush out and buy 'premature baby' clothes, as nothing we had prepared for her arrival fitted her tiny frame.

This renewed opportunity at parenthood came for me with a sense of freshness. I had raised my first two daughters as a single parent; this time I had a husband to raise our 'Gift from God' (the meaning of Shaun's name) and 'Beloved' (the meaning of Amy's name) with, yet I had no idea what that might look like, and so I sought sage advice from those around me who were faith-filled and had married and raised their children in more stable circumstances. From them, I received much wisdom and instruction in answer to my burgeoning questions. There is nothing quite like being led by the Holy Spirit, however, and as a new mother once again, I began to discover that the wisdom the Lord gave me directly was the best of all. I became especially aware and attuned to His voice as my Helper, often through my own children.

Around this time, I felt the Lord call me to leave my career. My husband was thrilled with the idea of me dedicating my time to full-time mothering. I too was filled with faith and enthusiasm that this was going to be such a good experience! Only, it wasn't that simple. I struggled with leaving the corporate world in exchange for nappies and a never-ending stream of laundry. Soon, I began to question whether I'd heard Him at all as I felt the insanity of staying at home all day beginning to crash in around me. It was just as I was questioning my decision and wondering if I should just head back to work, that my faithful Helper showed Himself to be real to me.

That particular day, I was baking biscuits with my almost three-year-old daughter when I asked God, 'Is this really what you want from my life? Is this what you saved me for? Biscuits!?' Surely, I figured, there was more to my life than this!

Right then, I then heard very clearly a voice say, *'Show them my ways.'* That was it, plain and simple—no discipleship class, no mother-care programs—just an instruction. What came next took me by surprise, but it changed my heart and gave me a love for being home that I could never have perceived for myself. Right there in the kitchen, my mouth opened and words began to flow forth from my spirit. I found myself explaining to my tiny baking apprentice that the porridge mix in the bowl was just like us, all crunchy and messy when we are full of sin. As we add the melted butter into the mess, it's just like when Holy Spirit gets added to our lives and we invite Jesus into our hearts.

Imagine my voice a few octaves higher than normal, the sound of a gentle fairy-mum pitch, as I began sharing these truths with her. It really was a very magical moment. Her little eyes widened with delight as the mixture formed and fell away from the sides into a recognizable biscuit mix and she got so excited! Just as I was ready to explain the transformation she bounced up and down squealing with sheer delight, 'It's a new creation, just like me!' Tears of joy welled up within me and began to gather in my eyes as I agreed wholeheartedly to her discovery and declared in agreement, 'Yes! Indeed, you are a new creation, just like the biscuit!'

As the day passed, my daughter happily sang, 'I'm a biscuit! I'm a biscuit!' to all who came across her path, bouncing about with absolute joy in the revelation. It remains memorable because it was so innocent and precious to behold. Let me remind you—never underestimate what God can do through you, even when you are almost three!

My little girl's absolute delight gave us many opportunities to share why she thought she was a biscuit as we went about our daily chores, and even the supermarket that day became a place where the good news of Jesus Christ was spread! God opened doors into hearts in ways I would never have imagined possible. My daughter encountered an elderly lady in the supermarket with her little song and we were able to pray with her for her heart to be filled with the same joy. It was a remarkable moment.

That was to be the first song of many yet to break forth from my little worship warrior, but I learnt more than one valuable lesson that day. God can move in amazing ways if we are willing to be led by His Spirit, and though the corporate world may be at times more stimulating for my brain, nothing can touch my heart like home.

That wonderful day opened me up to the possibilities of the gospel in my new environment, and I began to love being at home and being a mother even more because I understood the power of motherhood and the mission field God had given me. It was a gift to be raising these children in Christ and He had fully equipped and qualified me to do so. Motherhood had been restored to me and as I embraced my new position, another piece of my heart was being restored.

My life had been turned completely upside down and inside out; the woman I was no longer existed. She had been transformed by love, her broken heart was renewed, but the process to becoming whole of heart has a cost and is not easy. I was on a journey to wholeness by now.

People often tell me they can't imagine me as the person who is in the first chapter, calculated and ruthless, yet that is exactly where life had led me and where Jesus found me . . . in such a mess!

Through His word, He began revealing to me who I truly was in Him. And, He gave me a greater understanding of the gifts and anointing I held as a Seer. The more time I spent in His word the more I found myself settled and comforted in times of difficulty. The words on the pages began to take shape and form life right in front of my eyes. The deeper I searched, the more connected I felt. There is a richness in spending time alone with God through both good times and bad, and these are the moments I treasure continuously in my life still today.

You know, if it had been me that Jesus had met that day at the well instead of the Samaritan woman, the questions and answers would have been so alike. Jesus said to her, 'Go, call your husband,' to which she then replies, 'I have no husband.' He then goes on in that conversation to say, in effect, 'Well, you're right about that—you've had many more men, and the one you are with now is still not a husband.'

After facing her truth in the eyes of Christ, this incredible woman leaves that encounter to become the first woman evangelist, spreading the good news of this man and the truth He told. As a new believer, that same zeal had filled me. I just wanted everyone to see and feel Jesus in the same way I had. I wanted them to know He was as real today as he was then, that he was not just a story!

It was in this zeal that my husband and I had become Youth Pastors. Soon we decided to move closer to the church location so that we could more effectively reach into the local community. We sold our first home with relative ease and bought another just around the corner from the church. People were being healed in our church almost weekly and the power of God was moving mightily. Dreams and visions increased in our lives, and though the ability to hear from God still seemed a total phenomenon to us both, the accuracy with which we heard him was something we could not deny. What we were seeing Him do among us had become normal rather than unusual!

What we did not know, was that our faith was about to be tested in even greater measure. As the increase in power came, so did the persecution. Some of these things I cannot write about because they are not my story alone to tell. Not every soldier comes back from war and recovers—and that is true for the next phase of my journey. All I can say is that through immense personal pain, God provided pathways of hope to let me know He had not abandoned me. I was being fashioned into who I was created to be—a daughter of the King. The transformation however, was no easy thing for me; just as I seemed to be grasping the process, God continued to unexpectedly reshape every area of my life.

4

UNEXPECTED TRANSITIONS

Then, my husband had a dream that changed the entire course our lives. In his dream, he was flying what seemed to be a cargo plane between the North and the South Islands of New Zealand during the darkness of the night. As he flew the plane, he was praying, and with that came a sense of urgency within him to respond to the dream.

We didn't fully understand it at the time but as he shared the dream with me, he told me that he had gained his private pilot's license long before we met, but his eyesight had not been good enough to satisfy the requirements of a commercial license, so he had settled for recreational flying instead. This was a passion of his that I didn't even know about! Now, the unrealized dream within him began to rise. He wanted to fly again!

From my husband's dream, it seemed God had determined that my husband would fly again, only this time, he would fly commercial aircraft! I was in agreement with that too. For many years I had been focused on helping people discover their passion — I loved setting people on the path of their dreams wherever possible — so I encouraged my husband to look into the process of getting his commercial license and find out if it was possible. This is when the gift of faith I had been given really started activating! We had seen God do miracles already in our short time of knowing Him and knew that nothing was impossible. Now it was time for Craig to put this gift of faith to the test—and when he did, his eyesight was healed!

Now he met the requirements to train as a Commercial Pilot. The doors flung wide open as the Lord made a way where previously there truly had been no way. A training program that offered a full license with instrument rating on a student loan was available in the South Island of New Zealand. Moving there seemed the best option, since Craig had family and other contacts there too. Our home sold, a new enrolment place became available after another student dropped out, and suddenly we were off, leaving behind all we knew to forge a new pathway.

We arrived in Christchurch on the 7th of July, 2007. This seemed significant—when I looked it up, I learnt that the number 7 represents perfection and completion. Now, more than ever, I was convinced that we were following Gods lead. I knew this was God's perfect plan for us, and so off we went!

Oh my. If only I'd known how everything was about to change again. I was getting used to the rapid shifts of the Holy Spirit as he directed our steps forward in God's magnificent plan. Transition is not something I have historically been great with, but hindsight is a gift, and now it is clear to me that God was beginning my training early on! There was no doubt this new life we had chosen was full of surprises!

You wouldn't think that moving from one island of New Zealand to another would be too difficult—after all, we were not relocating to a completely different nation or culture, right? Suffice to say that the transition did not go as smoothly as expected. We landed in the South Island with great expectations, only to find that the level of faith we operated with was not something our South Island family knew of or had experienced. Even when we met several other believers who had similar faith journeys to ours, we found that they had either not encountered the Holy Spirit, or they believed that signs, miracles and wonders were a thing of the past. That took a bit of adjustment—and along the way, some feathers were definitely ruffled.

During the year that it took for my husband to gain his commercial license, I was home with four kids and no family to draw upon. With no close friends to lean into either, I turned to the Word of God, digging deeply into its pages, and enjoying glorious conversations with the Holy Spirit, my new 'best friend. When I look back over my journals from that time, I surprise myself at the amazing truths I uncovered in the Word during that season, and how much my relationship with God continued to deepen.

The loneliness of that time was devastating to both my heart and mind, but it was in this season that I genuinely began to find my worth as a daughter of the King. The time alone allowed me the freedom to search the scriptures and gave our family space to become a tightly knit unit, just the five of us together. At this time, the Holy Spirit began to lead me into a time of daily prayer and devotion. Little did I know that He was growing and positioning me for greater days ahead. Out of this time alone with Him came revelations, wisdom, and insight beyond my natural ability. I was beginning to develop some spiritual muscle, and this 'time out,' which had at first felt very harsh, swiftly turned into rock-solid training ground. I learnt so much about the power of prayer and the weapons of warfare in the spirit realms. I grew into a worship warrior and stepped out into fierce battles with the Lord at my side, determined to overcome the generational traumas and strongholds that had become fastened to my heart.

My life was a storehouse, hoarding years of wounds, but with every conquering victory came a great measure of the power that Jesus had deposited in me from the start! Layers of healing took place as the Holy Spirit led me and revealed my identity to me from the Word. I spent hours listening to worship and healing music, and reading autobiographies of those who had testimonies of overcoming. I was led by Holy Spirit to read many books on prayer and deliverance and as a result, my transformation made room for more of Jesus and the gifts of the Spirit—especially the gifts of wisdom and discernment.

Your ears shall hear a word behind you, saying,
'This is the way, walk in it,' whenever you turn to the right
hand or whenever you turn to the left.
Isaiah 30:21

Later that year, a visiting evangelist preached a sermon about hearing and heeding the voice of God. At that meeting, I received a prophetic word: 'Do *exactly* what Jesus did.' The speaker explained that Jesus did not *pray* for the sick, he *healed* them. He commanded a blessing and exercised His Kingdom authority. Now we get to do that in His name, as His representative here on Earth. 'When you have the Holy Spirit in you when you go to sleep, you 'glow-in-the dark' and demons flee!' he said. It made me giggle a little to think I might 'glow in the dark,' but I understood the magnitude of the power gift bestowed through that word and was left very encouraged.

Before moving to the South Island, I had turned down a job back home. Now, the same job miraculously appeared in this new city! This began my next phase of life—working within the mental health system in New Zealand. And to walk in this world, I was going to need everything God had taught me.

Soon, however, my husband's flying training was complete and we still did not know exactly what was next for us. After graduating, Craig found it difficult to get employment as a pilot. It seemed he needed to gain even more hours to reach the requirement most cargo services and smaller airlines wanted. Certainly, the dream of flying between the islands was not visible—in some ways, it seemed his dream had run out of runway without taking flight. By now, we had joined a local church, made new friends, and as we wrestled with God to understand clearly what the next step was for our future, we agreed we should settle for a life in Christchurch until we figured it out.

Remember my list at the very beginning of this book and my extremely selfish motivation at the time of seeking a man? Well it was as if Jesus was saying to me, *'Sharon, those desires weren't entirely selfish; your dream for your home is mine too, so here—I want to answer in abundance, beloved one.'*

I will never forget the day we moved into this mansion of a home. My grandfather had been taken to hospital, and things were not looking good. I was perched precariously on a pile of furniture, unloading our moving truck as the phone was handed up to me. I spoke briefly with him, he did not want me to race off to be with him, he wanted me to enjoy what he knew I had suffered and worked so hard for. This new home and everything it symbolized was my new start in so many ways. I loved my Grandad and we had a very close bond, but in that call, I discerned the words he wasn't saying. He was saying goodbye.

That was to be the last time we spoke, and though loss and a devastating crisis in the family had taught me how to get through with the help of the Comforter, I felt we had landed on our feet. We were cozy in our fabulous new home with our children around us. It was a house I never could have imagined living in, let alone owning, a true reward for all our losses.

But he said to me, 'My grace is sufficient for you, for my power is made perfect in weakness.' Therefore I will boast all the more gladly about my weaknesses, so that Christ's power may rest on me.
2 Corinthians 12:9

It was just when we were settled and feeling finally 'at home,' that Craig attended a men's conference and came home with a new burst of enthusiasm. 'I had a conversation with a man who heads up a mission organization,' he told me excitedly. And with those words, our family was catapulted on a pathway towards overseas missions.

It turned out that the organization were looking for pilots to fly in remote areas in the Pacific Region—Papua New Guinea, in particular. Craig felt an instant alignment with all that the man had shared, and although not every detail lined up with his original dream of flying between the two islands, still we sensed God was in it. This was the desire of Craig's heart—to fly and pray. And so, we began the application and vetting process and commenced Bible College training and missions-awareness workshops in order to fulfill the requirements and prepare for the way ahead.

Finally, my husband and I were in sync in our calling! We relished the long hours of study as we moved towards the goal of serving together again, this time, on the mission field. But the preparation time was disruptive for us as a family. A number of times we needed to travel to Australia to visit the organization's operational facilities, learn the logistics of homeschooling, and undergo further training in spiritual warfare. This was followed by support-raising, writing newsletters and then embarking on the 'missionary speaking circuit'—all before our posting had even been confirmed.

The venture was beginning to cost thousands of dollars before we had even got close to lift off, but we worked hard, did all that was required, and diligently sought the Lord and the wisdom of others along the way to confirm our direction. Eventually, we received a call—not to become a pilot family after all, but to fulfill an urgent need for an IT Manager in Papua New Guinea!

We were disappointed at first, but we took some time to work through this unforeseen change in roles, and, feeling sure that God was still in it, we said 'yes!' By now, we were ready to leave. Our flights out of Christchurch were lined up. We were on the doorstep of our last transition! And then, two massive earthquakes rocked our city in quick succession, putting all our plans on hold.

I could not believe it! Yet again, something just within our grasp was being snatched away. 'God,' I prayed, 'is my life meant to be such a roller-coaster?' It seemed the thief was back—only this time, the matter of my identity as a Daughter of the King had long been settled in my heart. I knew I was on a journey to become all that God intended me to be, and this new setback was no cause to doubt His love. Like the Samaritan woman, I had been set free from my past, renewed by faith, and felt ready to step out for something so much greater than myself. Surely this was not the end of the story! Yet still it seemed that every turn brought me inches from completing my assignment. Why did the goal posts have to keep moving?!

With the earthquakes came very hard times for us as a family. I had gotten used to being an overcomer in many areas of life by now and God had remained faithful throughout every trial. Still, trials and tribulations had almost become a permanent adversary, and the temptation to slip back into old behaviors was always there tugging at me.

It was not as if this road we had chosen to walk down as a blended family or as believers in Christ were all smooth; now, after laying it all down, we had suddenly been jolted out of our trajectory towards the mission field! The term 'baptism by fire' certainly felt very apt at this point of the journey. With the earthquakes came great loss and devastation, which we struggled to comprehend, along with the constant demand on our time and resources from others who had much greater and pressing needs.

We did what we could to be helpful and provide comfort where possible for those trying to make sense of the tragic loss of homes, life, and livelihoods whilst fighting a daily sense of guilt at times for surviving. It was a most traumatic time, and still to this day many have not recovered and perhaps never will.

Through this time, God took me to a deeper place of reflection regarding my own character and nature, especially around the subject of motherhood, and for the first time, I got to know the true 'mother-heart of God' as I was confronted with my own. My own internal belief systems still told me that I was not good enough, that I never would be, and that I was not worthy of anything better because of my own life choices. Now it was time to face those beliefs—to get to the root of what kept me held in bondage.

You see, although I had experienced some healing along the way, and although my character was being transformed, the intense pressure of survival during the earthquake recovery time caused deeper issues to surface in my life. In the past, I had been too afraid to go there, too scared of what I would find if I began to unravel the hurts of the past.

But the time had come. I could not run away any longer. I had become just like my mother—manipulating and controlling—and when one of my girls confronted me about that, it set off an absolute tirade of anger within me. My relationship with my mother had never been great, and it wasn't helped by her efforts to be helpful to me during my 'single mom' years. More often than not, I had been pushed aside, but since I relied heavily on her support during those years, I had given in and allowed her to have full control over my life and the kids.

All of that changed when I married Craig, and my mother became quite resentful. Surely moving to the South Island will help, I had told myself. Now, however, my daughter was raising a very real issue, and I realized, to my horror, that I had become the very person I had run from! History was repeating itself—and when my sixteen-year-old daughter decided in the aftermath of the earthquakes that she was leaving because of my control-issues, I knew I had some things to face up to. Now, the whole family was in distress.

And, the aftershocks kept coming. Our city was reeling, and so were we. In the midst of it all, my first grandchild was born and once again, the complications that arose sorely tested our faith. If we were to get through the horrific loss we had suffered as a community and as a family, and if my relationship with my daughter was to be resolved, I needed to get some counselling. It was time to address the learnt behaviors I had inherited.

Facing my need and capacity for mothering was difficult, but I had no choice. The earthquakes had unearthed my deepest vulnerabilities, and the only thing that made it all worthwhile was that it took me further on my journey as a Daughter of the King. Finally, I began to understand that God's original design for me was far more glorious, free and joy-filled than I had ever realized.

Around this time, my dad decided to come to relocate with his digger and truck to help with the relief efforts in Christchurch. This was an amazing time of healing and reconciliation for us both. Until now, we hadn't really resolved anything from when I left home as a teenager, and although we were friendly enough there was an unspoken rift and our relationship was a little strained—now, after all these years, a disaster had brought us back together, and we were able to settle our past and move forward, working together side by side as we ministered to our community. For two years, my father lived, dedicating himself to serving the community where we lived. This has now become a time I treasure and thank God so much for. Even amongst the hardest of times and the darkest moments there is always a light of hope.

So much of my teenage heart was healed through this time of reconciliation, and my relationship with my father was restored to a better place than it had ever been before. It would be because of this time that, not many years later, I would be able to stand and give my father's eulogy with wholehearted love for him. Had this time of serving together not taken place, I'm not sure I could not have done as well as I did.

5

BECOMING A DAUGHTER OF THE KING

2 Samuel 13 is a difficult and painful chapter. In it, we read the story of Tamar, the daughter of King David who was tricked and viciously raped by a brother. With her garments ripped to shreds, she is stripped bare and robbed of her mantle. Having entered his home wearing royal garments, she leaves clothed in shame. Then to top it all off, the brother who gives her refuge after she has been tossed into the street tells her to be quiet about the whole thing. Her father also does nothing to avenge her honor and there seems to be no justice for her.

Her brother Absalom does not want this unfortunate and sad event to take her peace, and so, he encourages her not to allow this moment to define her. 'Do not take this thing to your heart,' he says. In other words, 'Don't let this change you from the kind-natured, good-hearted girl you are into a hardhearted, bitter person.' He also tells her not to let anyone else know what has taken place, because the man who raped her was their brother. The best thing to do for the sake of family harmony, was to keep it to herself. Easy for him to say, you might think!

Gosh, does he have any idea what she's been through?! Can he even glimpse the sort of pain this has caused, and what has been stolen? Yes, he does. Later in the story this same brother avenges the honor of his sister Tamar, taking the life of the one who brought dishonor to her and their family, and as he takes his own path of retribution, he also faces the consequences for those actions with his own death.

Family dynamics can be complicated to navigate at times, and in my family of origin there were stories similar to Tamar's. The Holy Spirit had been cleaning up areas within my own heart, and in the process of bringing me through from brokenness to wholeness, the gaps in my memory began to heal, and with it, the story of my own sexual abuse as a child that had been deeply hidden in my own psyche.

Despite the counselling I had received, I still had no memories of my early childhood. To me, the ages of two to eight were a blank gap I had never been able to resolve. This is when my friend, the Holy Spirit, revealed to me in a dream what had taken place . . .

My 'family' as a child consisted of the friends my parents chose to become family. Now I recalled a couple who had been close friends in the early years of my life and then for some reason, dropped off the scene until I started college. At the time, I never thought it was odd—I was too young to consider any nefarious motives. But with the insight of the Holy Spirit, I remembered an incident when I was left alone with my 'uncle' while my mother was at work and had been molested! I also recalled how, as a girl in my first year of college, I was babysitting at their home, when the same man tried to climb into bed with me. I completely freaked out—only, I had never told anyone. Now, through a series of visions I was able to go back to the moment of the original abuse and I was supernaturally healed of the wounds and scars that event had left. This healing enabled me to walk in greater peace and understanding and opened my heart so I could begin to walk towards wholeheartedness rather than stay in the dark.

What I noticed most, however, as I read Tamar's account, was the absence of a mother in her story. She certainly had a mother—that was certain—but where was she, and what had she done about all of this? I began to question, where was my mother when my abuse happened? Did she know about it? Why hadn't she intervened? How had it become so hidden? I was so angry at my mother, so disgusted that as a mother she had done nothing! Maybe, if she had stopped it, I wouldn't have become such a promiscuous person! Maybe if she had stopped it, I would have retained my innocence! I was outraged at the thought.

It was a prophetic word I received at a conference that eventually unlocked the answers to my questions and caused my anger to subside. It was as if the Holy Spirit gently blew the panes of a window open, outward towards the scene of my abuse. He spoke softly to me: *'I'm going to show you what would have happened if your mother had intervened.'*

In my spirit, a scene unfolded as I saw what thankfully, had never happened. In my mind's eye, I saw my mother telling my father what had taken place. He then turned, found my abuser, and beat him so severely in his rage that he killed him. When the police arrived, my father was arrested and jailed for murder. How kind of God to show me why my mother had not stepped in. If she had, I would have been left without a father growing up. That day, the Holy Spirit told me that my mother knew exactly what my father was capable of and was afraid that his reaction would leave her and her friend both widows. In that case, my life would have been so much worse.

Instead, I had been spared that outcome. I had grown up with a loving father who, until my teens, I had a very close and loving relationship with; in fact, my mother often said I was the 'apple of his eye.' Now, rather than seeing only the injustice done to me by my mother's silence, I somehow understood what she as a mother had battled with. From that moment on, I stepped into a place of forgiveness and was released from the anger I held . . . and completely healed of the trauma! The bitterness I never realized I was carrying, left me in an instant.

God's favor in my life has always astonished me and just three years after the first earthquake hit, our house was repaired to a better state that when we had bought it. My dad finally retired and would have happily stayed in Christchurch, but we were ready to set off again towards Papua New Guinea. It was time for him to go home. And so, with the ink just dried on the sale agreement on our home, we were about to wave goodbye once again to all to embark on another transition.

Finally, we were heading off as missionaries to the people of Papua New Guinea. My husband had visited the country in the meantime and had fallen in love with both the people and the place. I had not seen him so excited since the night he came home from a concert to announce he was going to become a youth pastor! He was on fire — and I was in awe!

All of the reading I had done as a young girl had given me a great imagination; I had often dreamt that I would have adventures and travel the world, but it hadn't come to pass until I met Jesus! Shortly after my grandad passed away, I was able to live out one of those long-held desires when Craig arranged for me to take a break away. For four weeks, I travelled around England, Scotland and Canada, staying with friends and ministering along the way. Standing at the top of London Bridge, I raised my hands to the heavens and yelled, 'I made it, Grandad!'

But moving to Papua New Guinea was a whole other situation, and God had to do a work in my heart to get me to agree to take my children to a completely foreign culture with very few of the usual supports around us. Thankfully, I had learned that when God calls it is better to be obedient, because what awaits is His plan, which is pure joy!

Papua New Guinea wasn't exactly on my list of great places to visit, but it was on God's list for us, and with our granddaughter, who was almost eighteen months old and had now lived with us on a permanent basis, we left New Zealand to fly, via Australia, towards our new mission field.

As we approached the final leg from Port Moresby to Mount Hagen, I was already encountering things I had never seen before. I had been taught what to do if taken hostage, how to roll out of a moving vehicle or hide in scrub on the side of a road should I ever need to, but I now began to contemplate the same old question, 'What have I done this time?!'

'God,' I prayed as we began the descent for landing, 'when my feet touch the land, you have got to put a love in my heart for these people like you did for Craig. Please place a love in the heart of the people for me too, or we will never survive here.'

The welcome was something straight out of a movie. We were thrown with our suitcases into the back of two SUV's, with several others following after us and raced out of the airport onto a rough road, then bounced into a razor wired compound in what seemed like just a breath! This swift introduction of mayhem did nothing to reinforce any confidence in me that this was going to be a good time whatsoever.

We had arrived in the midst of general elections, which explained the need for such a dramatic arrival. It was not long, however, before Papua New Guinea turned into an amazing time for us as a family. We joined the local church, made friends with many national people and enjoyed the good weather as we watched faith arise more and more each day both in us and our community. There were many adventures during our stay, which, along with the miracles, signs and wonders we witnessed are the subject of another book.

Our stay in this glorious place was short lived for several reasons. One of those was that my husband and I had agreed that if our marriage or family looked remotely like it was falling apart, we would go home without reservation. We had heard of many missionary families breaking down on the mission field before we even left New Zealand, and we were determined not to become one of those statistics.

Now, however, Craig was working extremely long hours, and I was left at home alone with three small children, which in itself wasn't unexpected. Homeschool took up most of our day and then the kids were free to just play happily. The national people were wonderful to us all and accepted my children with open arms, even taking the youngest under their wing, so much so that I would often find her inside a local home helping herself to their homemade ice blocks!

But the different cultural values and religious beliefs within our compound were difficult to navigate, and I found it increasingly difficult to get along with some of the other 'white women.' One expat family struggled to understand my son who had been diagnosed with Asperger's Syndrome before we arrived. This made us feel a little like social outcasts and caused strain on our relationship with the mission agency too. But mostly, we were managing the many challenges of compound life in a culture so different to our own.

Then, apparently out of nowhere, my husband was struck down by a debilitating and agonizing illness. For almost a week, Craig was overcome with pain and was unable to eat. Constant diarrhea and vomiting were taking their toll on his body until, in the middle of one night, I determined that this was enough, we needed to get him to the mission hospital several miles away. Scared for how things were progressing, I called an older couple on the compound who assessed Craig and then arranged for a couple of men from the surrounding houses to transport him to hospital in a car. Hearing about how ill Craig was, his young apprentice, Max, insisted on accompanying him too.

I sat alone inside our house through that night while our three children slept. Furiously praying through my fears, I sent out a plea for help to our local church pastors and intercessors back home in New Zealand. I knew that the strength I lacked in the moment, God would provide through others.

My fears were not just for Craig, however. That night, as I looked out between the bars on the windows for any hint of his return, I was reminded why we lived in such security in the first place. Our compound was surrounded by razor wire fencing with glass shards concreted into the top of the fence line to stop any unwanted person from getting in.

I was thankful that Max was out there on the road with Craig. He was aware that the other men in the van were not at all pleased to have been be woken in the night hours regardless of their teammate's condition. It was a dangerous mission to drive at any time in the highlands of Papua New Guinea simply because of the poor state of the roads, but at night this was made worse by the possibility of being hijacked. John 15:13 says, *'Greater love has no one than this, than to lay down one's life for his friends.'* Max was such a friend. I later learned that Max prayed fervently all the way to the hospital, refusing to give in to what looked like death. He trusted God for a miracle, and back home, I too remained hopeful throughout my own tyranny of darkness.

Ravaged by dehydration and a soaring temperature, Craig was now beginning to encounter paralysis from the waist down. Was this just another stomach bug? Or food poisoning? One thing was certain—my husband was quickly fading away. The hospital staff conducted tests which also turned out to be inconclusive. Perhaps it was malaria, or dengue fever?

In any case, Craig was sent home several hours later with some medication and progressively he improved beyond the initial scare.

Three months later we were back in the same position, except by now we knew it was malaria, and thankfully, this time we knew what to do. A prayer team was quickly convened amongst our local church and national friends and as quickly as it came, it left. Knowing my authority, and supported by the renewed strength surrounding me, we pressed into battle and came out victorious!

Still, the bouts of illness had taken their toll . . . and exposed our vulnerabilities in other areas. I was burdened by the reality that I was not getting on with our teammates, and that, along with the feeling that my children were a burden to others, had made me bitter. Knowing that my mental health would only get worse if we kept living in this type of social isolation, and seeing the pressure it added to our already-strained marriage, we made the difficult decision to cut our four-year term short.

We were deeply sad and felt like we had failed on so many levels. We had been so certain of our calling; now it seemed as if all our investment of time and money had been wasted. Had we got it wrong? The disappointment that Craig would not be there to oversee all his plans for improving the infrastructure weighed heavily on us. And, we knew that, without Craig there to train him, Max, his faithful apprentice, would lose his job.

But we had come to the end of ourselves. My husband was still very weak from his second bout of malaria, and was barely able to walk when we boarded the plane to leave. As we prepared for takeoff, I could hear the wailing outside. Peering through my tears, I looked out of the window. Our tribe and national friends were running down the side of the runway as they waved goodbye. Our hearts were broken. God had put his true love for the people of Papua New Guinea in our hearts, and all I could hope was that one day we could return to embrace them all once again.

The ministry portion of our time in Papua New Guinea had been marked by the miraculous—now, however, we were returning home with our heads hung low, full of pain and mixed emotions. But that would have to wait. For now, we just needed somewhere to live. We were relieved when some friends in Christchurch told us they were heading overseas for a year and needed someone to care for their home. In God's timing our schedules fitted together perfectly, and we were able to move in.

But despite the fact we had only been gone a year or so, we had returned as very different people. The lens through which we viewed the world had changed, and we seemed to have no purpose. It didn't take long before the wheels began to fall off. We were home in Christchurch, but we had nothing—no jobs, no house (we had sold it before we left), no furniture, and after a few weeks, no financial supporters either.

Now we were back to being on 'the benefit,' Craig was becoming depressed, and then we discovered our youngest child was partially deaf! Still homeschooling, I knew I had to keep going, but I was battle weary myself, and just exhausted from it all.

Hope deferred makes the heart sick, but when the desire
comes, it is a tree of life.
Proverbs 13:12

Our changeover back into New Zealand life soon smoothed out, but over time we began to face the disillusion and disappointment we had encountered on the mission field. We had given everything we had to go, selling all that we owned or giving it away. We had left our families and our community in the midst of the ongoing relief and recovery from the ever-present aftershocks that continued in Christchurch for seven years after the first event. We had responded to the call of God to live in another land, learn another language and become part of another community that God loved, and we had come to love them too.

Now we—and others—were left brokenhearted. Where had we gone wrong? Had we misinterpreted Gods lead? What did we miss? Why had it been so difficult and yet so miraculous all at the same time? We had hundreds of questions, and we wrestled through them with ourselves, each other, and God. It was as if the joy we had known in His service was being sucked out of us piece by piece until eventually there were hardly any pieces left. In the homecoming, we had lost our joy, and by the time we finally settled, we were emotionally wrecked.

Back home on familiar ground and blindly optimistic, we expected things would improve over time. But what we didn't realize was that, although Craig and I had agreed that we needed to come home, our marriage was now on very shaky ground because of that decision. We had made a stand together, but now the conviction of that decision was being tested. Our strength as a couple was being stretched, and although on the outside things seemed fine, on the inside we were hanging together by a very thin thread. Counselling helped us a little as we worked through all we had experienced and tried to bring the pieces of what we had lost back together. Even so, the truth of 'hope deferred' overflowed our emotional river and flooded our already weakened state.

We went back to our home church, but we were too broken to take in or take on anything that was really happening during that first year; we were aware, however, that while we had been gone, our church had also struggled and was on the brink of an uncomfortable split. In our damaged heart-space, we had no capacity to cope with issues at church as well, and soon lost all desire to be there.

God had always been faithful; now, however, it seemed that everything we had thought we were coming back to was crumbling all around us—our city, our church, our marriage, our hope. If we were to recover, we needed to spend time rebuilding our relationships with God, each other, our children and our community.

With the help of counselling services, our marriage was recovered before it was too far gone, but it did come very close. Although we had successfully celebrated ten years of marriage and even renewed our vows in Papua New Guinea, coming home had meant facing a lot of character issues that were very tough to come to grips with. This was a time where I had to stand before God in all my inability and vulnerability and face up to issues I had previously avoided and those I was unaware of that had been lurking in the darkness of my mind and heart. Nothing was the same after we came home, and realistically, nothing could stay that way either.

As part of our journey together, Craig and I began to realize that along the way, we had become more dependent on each other than we had on God—and this was affecting our marriage. Now it was time to step into a new place of dependency on God rather than each other, and as we did, we found ourselves going deeper in our faith than we had ever gone before. By now we had found a new home to live in, and once again pushed the restart button, but a pattern had formed in our lives, and sure enough, just as we seemed to be getting back onto solid ground, the very ground I was standing on was whipped out from under my feet as I encountered yet another betrayal. It seemed my journey to becoming the daughter and woman of God I so desired to be was still fraught with challenges.

6

OUT OF THE PIT

*'If that is the case, our God whom we serve is able to deliver us
from the burning fiery furnace, and He will deliver us from
your hand, O king.'*
Daniel 3:17 NKJV

When I first came to know Jesus, I had no expectations whatsoever of what a life with faith might look like. Over the years, however, I had unwittingly built some unrealized expectations. No one ever sold me a sweet version of the Gospel, but neither did I expect such a roller coaster of life. Despite the ups and downs of life's adventures I still knew God had been with me in every storm. He was refining everything in me to become all I was predestined to become in Him and although my spirit knew we were heading for complete and total freedom it took a while to break through and change some of those patterns. Although my mind was being renewed on a daily basis breaking old thinking, old habits and learnt responses my soul took a while to catch up with my spirit.

I had already experienced so much transformation in my own life and witnessed the miraculous power of God in transforming others, but as

I began to face this next phase of my character makeover, something new emerged from within me. The creative gifts that had laid untapped within me began to rise in a greater measure than I ever knew existed.

As I worked through my pain and heartache, the Seer gift was being awoken within me in greater measure than before and I began to see and hear things as my spiritual senses increased. When visions came to my mind, I quickly discovered that painting what I saw was the best way to express them. I had no experience of being a painter and no clue how to go about it, but I fumbled with tracing images onto canvas and mixing messy paint pots.

Then, one day I literally asked the Holy Spirit to help me paint. Suddenly, paintings began to emerge! I started using painting as a way to work through the pain I was experiencing, to process some of the uglier aspects of life that had surfaced. As I painted with Him, it felt like the Lord was taking a surgical knife to my heart, replacing the dark areas with His light, uprooting the narcissistic characteristics that had rubbed off in my childhood and setting me free. This was a gradual process of dying to self—hard, but necessary, and painting enabled me to go through it.

As I healed, I found myself able to bring to the canvas what I had seen in the heavenly realms, and as God began to teach me, I found that each painting came with a promise. During my very first painting, the Lord me gave a special promise: *'I am breaking every chain.'* This verse from Isaiah 61 speaks of setting the captives free from the darkness that holds them; it speaks of exchanging beauty for ashes and a garment of praise for the spirit of heaviness.

In the end, what I thought was a descent into the abyss of darkness, was really a deliverance experience. I cannot pinpoint exactly one thing that led to what could be easily described as a breakdown of sorts, but I can tell you I felt like I had slipped into a great expanse of nothingness. A void existed in my life and everything had gone quiet.

I had just left a prayer gathering when, as I was driving down the road, I had a vision of myself lying naked at the bottom of a deep pit surrounded by fine gravel on the dirt beneath me. It looked like I had fallen down a dark well, and I was curled up in a fetal position. Above me, I could hear people walking around and talking. The gravel underneath me was rough against my bare skin and made my squirm. Somehow, I knew I was meant to be there though, so I wasn't afraid at all. But I couldn't possibly understand the vision and why on earth I would be 'put' in such a place. I knew somehow that God was responsible for this, that He had put me here, but *why*? This pit was a far cry from the heights of glory I believed I was predestined for, and in that moment, shame covered me like an itchy woolen blanket.

In my vision, I felt very exposed. Annoyed at God for leaving me in such a state and in what seemed such an unforsaken place, I began to yell, crying out to the Lord, '*I'm naked down here! Hello! Can't you see!? All those people can see me, you know! Don't you know how terrible this is for a woman, to be laid naked like this?*'

A soft, gentle breath whispered over me with astonishing kindness in the reply, '*You are not seen by anyone but me. No one can 'see' you, and you are not alone . . . I am with you. The reason you are naked is because you have been stripped of everything that has held you back and hinders you from*

coming closer to me. Now there is nothing between you and me. When you are
ready to stand back up again, I will clothe you in new garments.'

As quickly as it had arrived, the vision ended, and I found myself
pulling into my driveway unable to remember the streets I had just
driven down! To this day I have no idea how I drove the distance from
that meeting to home! I remained in the car for a while with my mouth
open in awe at what had just taken place, trying to grasp what I had
seen and heard.

From that point on, however, the chains began to break off my life one
by one, just as God had promised me from the first painting—chains
that represented events, situations or relationships that had bound me
to ways of living.

In my case, the first chain that got severed was the chain of
unhealthy, toxic relationships. At the time I could not
understand why so many of my relationships were coming
apart. Having moved cities and then countries, it was
surprising how many people had moved on in such a short time. But in
the process of leaving the local church that we had returned to, I had
experienced accusations, gossip, and a deep betrayal by a friend. With
church no longer feeling like a safe place, and with nothing resolved, I
mourned as those ties were broken.

With hindsight I could see that my dependence on someone for
friendship and the breakdown that followed was a catalyst that
bought me closer to God and increased my relationship with Him. It
was only years later, after God had amazingly worked in both of us,
that the healing power of His love brought us back together to become
united in His purposes. Now, that relationship is better than ever
before, and all is forgiven.

The next chain to be broken was an inner vow I had made with myself to put my spiritual gift of a 'Seer' on the shelf. I had always 'seen' or 'known' things that were often beyond my own ability or understanding and had no explanation for why that was. From my first encounter with Jesus, I had begun to see more clearly in the spirit realm. But no one around me at the time understood it well enough to be able to walk with me in the development of that gift. Besides, some of the things I started seeing and sensing frightened me.

When we begin to walk in spiritual gifts, it can become very overwhelming. Now, the Holy Spirit showed me that I had made an inner vow—one that I was completely unaware of. While I had thought I was simply putting this gift on the shelf, what actually took place was a re-routing by the enemy who wanted to steal my destiny and shut down this gift in my life. In my state of weakness and with a lack of people who were spiritually mature and discerning in my life, I had mistakenly made an agreement to 'shelve' this gift.

Now was the time for that agreement to be broken. So, in an act of repentance and submission I took myself before the Lord and asked for forgiveness for not stewarding my gift well, and once again His grace abounded. Immediately I began operating in my gifting again, this time, in an even increased way. The gift may have been paused for a time, but it never went away. Be encouraged in this that when God gives you a gift, it remains!

With my spiritual sight restored and the fears that held me in bondage now smashed, I began to hear and see the spiritual realm more clearly. As my 'Seer' gift increased, I enrolled in a prophetic class so that I could learn how to minister this gift. Soon, I was creating more and more paintings as the gift in me was released through my paintbrush!

I have come to believe that we are all creative people, that we possess the qualities of our Creator all the time! I had never had professional training or lessons in *how* to paint and yet somehow, I had this ability to bring life to a canvas in an abstract fashion. I soon realized that it wasn't even actually me that was painting, that the Holy Spirit had assigned angels to produce His works, simply allowing me to put my name upon the finished pieces as we co-created magnificently together. It became a dance of sorts and out of that space flowed the heavenly revelation.

The artistic unravelling in a time of self-mourning had become my road into untapped creativity. It was as if God had provided a way where there seemed no way; that if I were to get out of the pit I was in, I needed to use my gift and paint my way out! A piece of me that was lost had been found and reawakened.

 The next chain came with many links—a chain of authority. The Holy Spirit showed me that this chain did not require breaking—it needed to be put back together! The authority dynamics I had encountered on the mission field and on my return home, had knocked me hard. The next painting I created was a mixed media work of a figure carrying a limp body through a chaotic scene. I was wounded by authority, but I was coming to a place of safety. And once again, the painting came with a promise that God was with me.

God speaks to us all in different ways. It was when I was on a road trip with some artistic friends that I walked into a cosmetic store, and as I was looking at the perfumes, I heard a voice say, *'Beautiful.'* I turned around in astonishment, but no one was there. As I looked up, however, I saw before me, on the wall display, a clear bottle with one word written on it—*Beautiful*.

I walked to the other side of the store trying not to burst out into uncontrollable tears. The love of God I felt for me in that moment was beyond words. I was so humbled. The Holy Spirit then prompted me to buy the perfume. *'This is for you, you're a beautiful fragrance unto the Lord,'* He said. I didn't have enough money to buy that particular bottle but next to it was another perfume labelled 'Faithful,' and it was affordable, so I purchased that instead. It was true. God had been so faithful toward me.

Not long after I left the store, however, I felt very uncomfortable with my purchase. When I told my friend what had happened and that I'd made a mistake, she said, 'Oh my goodness, yes! We must go back right now!' She then told me while she was in the store, she had felt she was supposed to buy that perfume for me, but because I had selected a different one, she was unsure if she had heard correctly! We laughed at each other and managed to exchange the perfumes . . . and the shop assistant even charged me the same price for the larger bottle as for the smaller bottle I had bought! It was as if God had changed the price tags while we had been gone!

Suddenly a boldness that was not my own came over me. Noticing the shop assistants' necklace, I made a comment on it, and immediately she began to tell me her life story! She was of Jewish decent, she shared, and had come to New Zealand to live. Unfortunately, things had not gone so well for her here as she had hoped.

I shared with her about the perfume, what God had spoken to me, and why I had come back to the shop. The shop remained empty the whole time as we talked openly about Jesus and then prayed together. When I left, if was with so much more than perfume in my hand! I left that day knowing that I can always trust Gods leading for both my good and for His glory!

There is a passage of scripture in the Song of Solomon, that, when I read it, I feel as if it is alive! It runs off the pages dripping with such extravagant love all over me, as if the very words are singing to me: 'My beloved speaks and says to me: "Arise, my love, my beautiful one, and come away, for behold, the winter is past; the rain is over and gone"' (Song of Solomon 2:10).

That week away on tour was an amazing time of revelation and discovery. God had begun to restore the broken areas within my heart with new relationships, friends who brought life to my bones as well as encouragement to my spirit. When I returned home, I found a group of people who understood the spiritual realms. These people lovingly fostered me in and nurtured me back to spiritual health. The cold, dark 'winter' I had experienced was over and now it was time to rebuild the areas of light within me. I began to rise once more, this time, with my heart firmly anchored in love.

Over the years, despite the broken relationships, God brought people to my side to hold me up when I could not uphold myself. Those who have silently prayed for me have been my strongest asset. One of those was a lady who had been a dedicated intercessor whilst we served overseas and remained faithful in her prayers for me and my family as we transitioned back to New Zealand. She spent time with me— praying, encouraging, painting (even though she had never done it before herself)—and, she gently suggested I take time to just read autobiographies and novels for a while. What timely advice! Through reading stories, real and imagined, I learned to reflect and be calm; I learned to sit with God more, and to hear from Him in a new way.

One morning as I painted, a garment began to appear on my canvas. Within it was wrapped a woman who looked so strong, bold and confident, but it wasn't me. I called her 'the Intercessor' at first because she sat with a large blanket around her shoulders, positioned in such a way that was relaxed, but at the same time determined. Diamond earrings dripped from her ears, and a diamond necklace adorned her neck. I found her gaze striking, and as she was formed in the paint strokes, I knew that she was a representation of the strength of the woman God had created in all His daughters, including me. It took me a while to understand why this woman gripped me so much—her whole mannerism, her entire being spoke of and exuded authority. As I sat with this painting and prayed, God highlighted to me that an exchange was about to take place, that I was to come into greater authority.

But then came a warning: *'You can't run or hide any more. It is time to face the truth and we will do it together. I'm sorry it will be painful, but it will be quick, and I will be with you.'* Then I had a vision where I saw myself going over broken glass down on my knees, but as I lifted my head, I could see light at the end and it was close by, just as the Lord had spoken.

What followed was nothing short of a two-week journey into the supernatural miracle-realms. I had enough faith to believe that the promise of God to be with me was true, and I held onto it tightly as the Holy Spirit led me through a complete cleansing of my spirit, soul and body. This extraordinary process took me through each room of my physical home. In each room, the Lord gave me a scripture, a song, and a promise, breaking generations of iniquity off me as I scrubbed from ceiling to floor.

The end of this cleansing process found me sitting under a prayer shawl which had been given to me by a dear friend who had visited Jerusalem. As I was relishing the moment of basking in God's glory that morning, a familiar whisper told me to run and take a photo of myself under this garment. I was quick to obey the command, and when I looked at that photo, I cried and cried. I could not believe it was my own reflection looking back at me. The woman I saw was truly *beautiful!*

I could not stop looking at that photo for the longest time. I could hardly recognize myself at all. Even my husband didn't recognize me when I showed it to him! I really did look magnificent! It took a while for me to get comfortable with my 'new look,' but I knew that from here on in, I would walk with new garments, royal robes of authority, and that the beauty of the Lord would be upon me. I watched as justice came with recompense for all I had lost and that which had been stolen started to be returned. The Lord had indeed given me 'beauty for ashes' (Isaiah 61:3). He had taken my grieving and turned it back to joy, just as He had promised.

God in His great mercy and love had retrieved every lost part of me, restoring each piece so tenderly and with such love that I was no longer the broken vessel I had proclaimed to be. Now I was a complete vessel, restored to the original design my Creator had always intended for me.

From tragedy to triumph, from redemption to recovery . . . that has become my story. It's not the journey I dreamed of as a teenager, and I'm sure it's not the story God originally wrote for me either. My choices determined the twists, turns and even the detours of my path. Life takes its turns, and sometimes we make what we think are the best choices in the moment only to find that they don't always work out for our best.

Rahab was a woman who, like many of us, had plans and dreams in her youth that never quite seemed to work out. As I reflect upon her story in Joshua 2, I find that she and I have much in common.

I've often wondered what lead her into a life of prostitution. What was her situation? What were her goals in life? What twists and turns did her pathway take on the road to redemption? How did she get into the predicament she finds herself in when two spies enter her home? It makes me wonder about the choices she had to make along the way, and how they took her from being a prostitute to being a completely transformed woman—a heroine even?

Rahab's journey is a lesson in great courage despite overwhelming circumstances. She knew there was a better life than the one she was living, and when she recognized the opportunity for greater freedom, she plucked up the strength to take it wholeheartedly. In the process, she went from being enslaved to being set free—free indeed! Rahab accepted a God she had only heard of before, and in so doing, her life was redeemed, she was made new, her sins were forgiven, and she could start afresh.

This is the same offer I had been given, and it is the same offer that is available to you today. You too have the opportunity to choose! My life has not been exceptional, I have not had to overcome huge adversity, but I have endured years of decisions with painful consequences and a lot of grief. Grief can be such a hidden emotion, and it plays out differently in each circumstance, but God promised me 'joy instead of mourning' (Isaiah 61:3) and he offers that to you as well.

Even though I, like Rahab, had been set free, the adjustment from a life lived for the wrong purposes to a life lived for God is gradual. It takes time for the process of transformation to stick. No matter how great our new life is, it is often difficult to let go of what we know and embrace the possibilities that lie ahead, especially when we may not even understand them yet. It was only when I gained a solid understanding of my true identity as a child of God and my authority as a believer that I was ready to step out, clothed in the royal robes of a Daughter of The King!

One day, as I was writing this book, I sat on a beach and felt God was saying, *'See the ebb and flow of the waves on the beach, Sharon? They represent the tides of your life. There have been seasons, and some waves were higher and crashed more than others. There have also been times of gentle coming and going amongst the storms and the waves, but I have always been with you through the rise and the fall of each situation.'*

There are many 'kings' we may identify with in this world. Becoming a daughter of 'the King,' however, involves finding and claiming our identity in Christ. It often takes a journey of discovery to believe the truth about who God says we are and to walk in that truth. The lie of this world was that I was not good enough, that nothing I did would ever measure up. The truth of living in this world as a daughter of the King is that I am more than enough for God and that I am good!

I did not walk alone; these three women in the Bible—the Samaritan woman, Tamar, and Rahab—helped me along the journey. All three experienced excruciating pain, isolation from their own communities, tragic humiliation and loss. Yet all these women became daughters of the King as God transformed each one in His own way.

Now I want to leave you with this same hope—not a *glimmer* of hope, but a *promise* of hope. You too, can have a 'Redemption story.' God can rewrite the pages of the script that the enemy dealt you just as He did for me. God promises in John 10:9 that all who believe in Him shall be saved. Today is your opportunity to do just that. I urge you to believe! It is my prayer that as this book touches your life, you would simultaneously be given the gift of hope and faith, and that you would know how much God loves you and how possible it is for your life to be transformed.

AN INVITATION

If this book has resonated with you in any way and you now feel ready for a life of transformation from the place you find yourself in today to the place you are designed and destined for, I invite you to pray this prayer with me:

God,
Today I turn my heart towards You. I acknowledge that Jesus Christ is Your Son and that He died on the Cross and rose again, overcoming death, so that I may live. I repent of my sins and ask for Your forgiveness. Renew in me a right spirit and create in me a clean heart, Lord, and fill me today with Your Holy Spirit.
Amen

Acts 16:30-33
And he brought them out and said, 'Sirs, what must I do to be saved?' So they said, 'Believe on the Lord Jesus Christ, and you will be saved, you and your household.' Then they spoke the word of the Lord to him and to all who were in his house. And he took them the same hour of the night and washed their stripes. And immediately he and all his family were baptized.

You are now a new creation and have been set free! I encourage you to find a local church or fellowship and become strengthened in your decision by being baptized with water as you follow Christ.

AUTHOR'S NOTE

This account of my journey is just the beginning, there are many more stories dwelling within me that God wants me to write and share so that many may know Him. Since becoming a 'Daughter of the King' I have gone on to have adventures with Christ all over the world. I look forward to sharing more of God's story in me with you in the next book.

RECOMMENDED RESOURCES

Supernatural Childbirth
by Jackie Mize

Jesse: Found in Heaven
by Chris Pringle

Seeing the Supernatural
by Jennifer Eivaz

Glory Carriers
by Jennifer Eivaz

Healing the Wounded Soul
by Katie Souza

ACKNOWLEDGEMENTS

To **Craig Reynolds**—my husband, my biggest supporter, and my greatest fan always. Thank you for your commitment to pick up your cross and love me daily.

To **my children**—Jessica, Catherine, Lydia, Daniel, Shaun and Amy. Thanks for being such cool kids!

To **my first Pastors, Gwyn and Chris Slatter** of Hosana World Outreach Centre in Lower Hutt, New Zealand. Huge thanks to you both for all your discipleship and support in the beginning of my walk with Christ. Thank you for giving me firm foundations of faith.

To **Pastors Lorraine and David Rua** of Zoe Life Ministries in Selwyn, New Zealand. Thank you for your care, love and genuine support as spiritual parents. You truly are the unconditional love of Christ in all ways. Thank you for believing in me.

To **my mentor, Pastor Jennifer Eivaz** of Harvest Church, California, USA. Thank you for giving voice to the Seer gift with such ease and for releasing so many into their callings and setting them free from oppression that held them back. Your genuine love and goodwill towards all is to be admired and followed. Thank you for allowing me to glean and grow under the safety of the wing you have provided.

I would to acknowledge and sincerely honor **Anya McKee**, my editor. In bringing this book to life, Anya has faithfully guided me, keeping you, the readers, in mind at all times without losing my voice at all— she gets me! —and for that, I remain extremely thankful.

Whaea Sharon Reynolds leads The HIVE NZ Ltd., impacting nations with her innovative programs, ideas, expertise and leadership. She is a creative entrepreneur, an exhibited artist, an accomplished writer as well as wife, mother and grandmother based in Christchurch, New Zealand. Whaea (pronounced *Fire*) is an indigenous Maori word that has multiple meanings and is a title given to Sharon by her people as a leader and mother to the nations. Sharon is of Ngati Kahangunu and Te Arawa descent.

Whaea Sharon's work as a Community Arts Therapist has taken her into the high schools and prisons of Aotearoa and Africa, and into Cambodia where she has worked with children rescued from trafficking. Her unique programs and workshops use mixed modalities that offer hope. She works to bring justice to those who live with injustice, and to see people and communities transformed by the love and redeeming power of Christ.

To connect with Sharon or to enquire about speaking engagements, please email sharon@thehivenz.org

CPSIA information can be obtained
at www.ICGtesting.com
Printed in the USA
LVHW020454021120
670427LV00006B/1123